Plant-Based Cooking for Two

Plant-Based Cooking for Two

80 Deliciously Easy Whole-Food Recipes

Sara Speckels, NBC-HWC

Photography by Darren Muir

ROCKRIDGE PRESS

Interior and Cover Designer: Jami Spittler
Art Producer: Meg Baggott
Editor: Rebecca Markley
Production Editor: Dylan Julian
Production Manager: Eric Pier-Hocking

Photography © 2021 Darren Muir. Food styling by Yolanda Muir
Author photo courtesy of L.L. Eveland

Paperback ISBN: 978-1-63807-945-3 | eBook ISBN: 978-1-63807-269-0
R0

For my mother, Janet:
You taught me how
to cook when I was five.
You have given me my world—
and it is scrummy.

Sweet Potato and Black Bean Burgers 73

CONTENTS

INTRODUCTION

Plant-based eating has completely taken the food world by storm. From celebrity chefs creating eggplant "steaks" that go viral to fast food companies jumping on the plant-based bandwagon by adding vegan burgers to their menus, it's impossible to deny that eating more plants is going mainstream, and for good reason.

Choosing to eat more plants instead of animal products has undeniable health, environmental, and animal rights benefits. But with the sudden rise in popularity of plant-based diets comes a lot of confusion and frustration. Take me, for example: I'm proud to say I've been living and thriving with my plant-based lifestyle and coaching others on how to live healthier lives for more than a decade. But that transition from an adventurous, anything-goes foodie and chef to a plant-based National Board Certified Health and Wellness Coach wasn't all sunshine and roses, not in the least. Nevertheless, adopting a plant-based lifestyle has, admittedly, been the most important decision I've ever made. It has shaped my career, my health, my life, and the lives of others in ways I could have only imagined when I was younger.

When I was a young cook and restaurateur, food became my passion, my livelihood, and, some might say, my obsession. To call me a "foodie" was the understatement of the century. But this foodie lifestyle came with a price. I developed several chronic health issues in my mid-30s and I could no longer deny that the food choices I was making were destroying my health and my quality of life. As result, I adopted a simple motto: *Eat less processed junk. Eat more whole plants.* Eight simple words; what could be easier, right? With the power of hindsight, I woefully underestimated how challenging that transition would be.

Even though I had been cooking personally and professionally for three decades, I still ended up not really knowing what to cook and eat if my meals weren't centered around oil, meat, eggs, and dairy. Classic cooking techniques, like blooming spices in oil or adding copious amounts of cream, butter, and eggs, were what I knew. Without those techniques and ingredients, I made boring, inedible, and flavorless bowls of mush. I struggled to find a way to make food delicious AND healthy. Not only that, but whenever I found plant-based recipes online or in cookbooks, the recipes always served a crowd of six or more, and I was left with tons of uninspired leftovers that just rotted in the fridge.

Whether you're an "empty nester" wanting to prepare precisely portioned meals for you and your partner, a newlywed couple looking to find quick and easy meals for two tailored to a busy lifestyle, or someone who wants to introduce the exciting flavors and health benefits of plant-based cooking into your life, this is the book for you. I've removed the guesswork, frustration, and waste that so often comes with making this transition and carefully crafted a set of recipes that are quick, easy, healthy, and most important, delicious.

Plant-Based Cooking for Two: 80 Deliciously Easy Whole-Food Recipes is here not only to give you healthy and delicious recipes, but also to provide the tips, knowledge, and tools you'll need to plan, shop, prepare, cook, and enjoy eating more whole plants. I hope you're as excited as I am that you're reading this book. Let's dive in, get set up for long-term success, and start this plant-based journey together, one delicious and perfectly portioned meal at a time.

Chapter One

PLANT-BASED AS A PAIR

ARE YOU TIRED OF COOKBOOKS with recipes large enough to serve an army when you're cooking only for one or two? Are you bored with eating the same meal six nights in a row, or feeling guilty when throwing away a mountain of spoiled leftovers? Well, my plant-curious friend, this is the book for you. I welcome you to the exciting and flavorful world of plant-based cooking for two. Whether you've been cooking and eating plant-centered meals for years or are completely new to cooking and preparing your own meals, this book is designed to help you stop wasting your time, money, and groceries on enormous recipes and start cooking easy and flavorful plant-based meals for just two people.

Get Healthy Eating Plants, Together

You might be asking the question: "What does eating 'plant based' really mean?" I get it; these days, you'll likely hear people use words such as "vegetarian," "vegan," and "plant forward." Terms like "Meatless Monday" and "flexitarian" are becoming increasingly popular, which can make this all a little confusing. So, let's specify what we're talking about.

Although vegetarians choose to avoid eating meat, they do still eat animal products such as dairy, eggs, and honey, to name a few. They may also eat highly processed foods like fried tater tots. Plant-forward and flexitarian individuals are considered vegetarian and are typically focused on wholesome plants in an effort to improve the overall quality of their diets, but may still include some animal products. Vegans, on the other hand, avoid ALL animal products, including other nonfood animal products, like wool, silk, or leather goods, as part of a lifestyle choice. Still, vegan foods can be highly processed (think: French fries and diet soda!) and that's an important distinction—just because a food doesn't contain animal products and is considered "plant based" doesn't make it automatically healthy.

This book combines the best of both worlds: These recipes contain NO animal products, but also use only unprocessed and minimally processed ingredients and contain only small amounts of added salt, oil, and refined sugar. But I like to focus on all of the foods you CAN eat, instead of the few you don't. There are literally thousands of beans, fruits, nuts, seeds, vegetables, and whole grains to choose from. Also, with the increased interest in plant-based eating in recent years, there are MANY more plant-based choices available than there used to be, even in restaurants! Millions of people are doing it, sustaining it, and thriving on it. And these recipes will jump-start you toward making this way of eating healthy, realistic, and sustainable, while still bursting with flavor.

The Principles of Plant-Based Eating

Now that you're familiar with some of the benefits of a plant-based diet, let's take a moment to break down this book's three main principles.

EAT PLANTS AND ONLY PLANTS

Despite what the meat and dairy industries may have led you to believe, a well-planned, diverse plant-based diet can provide the nutrients your body needs to thrive. Grains, legumes, and vegetables contain the protein and all the essential amino acids you need. Dairy products aren't required for calcium; beans like edamame and white beans; green leafy vegetables like spinach, bok choy, and

Benefits of a Plant-Based Diet

Here are just a few reasons people are eating more plant-based meals and the benefits this way of eating can bring to you, your health, and our planet:

OUR PLANET. Did you know that the meat industry generates nearly 20 percent of the human-made greenhouse gas emissions that cause climate change? Plus, beef requires about 900 gallons of water to produce an 8-ounce steak, whereas vegetables use, on average, only about 20 gallons of water to produce 8 ounces of food. Centering your meals on plant foods can greatly cut your carbon footprint and reduce the amount of water your food needs to grow by 55 percent.

YOUR GUT MICROBES. Do you know who loves fiber? Your gut microbes. Despite all the hype about dairy yogurt's probiotics, feeding your gut's microbes a diet filled with fiber-rich, prebiotic plant foods is even more successful at building and nurturing a healthy and diverse gut microbiome.

YOUR HEALTH. A wholesome plant-based diet has been proven to help lower cholesterol, reduce the chances of developing certain types of cancer and chronic illnesses such as type 2 diabetes, and reverse and prevent heart disease.

YOUR IMMUNE SYSTEM. Vitamin C, found in bell peppers, Brussels sprouts, and strawberries, to name a few, helps keep your immune system strong.

YOUR LIFESTYLE. Most fad and crash diets, like juice cleanses, meal-replacement shakes, and low-carb diets, leave you feeling deprived and bored, while relying heavily on restricting calories and eating prepackaged foods. Fad diets just aren't sustainable for most people. Make no mistake, though, plant-based eating is NOT just another fad diet, but rather a healthy and sustainable lifestyle you can enjoy and follow for many years to come.

YOUR SKIN. Foods high in antioxidants (such as vitamins A, E, and C) like almonds, avocados, spinach, and sweet potatoes, help wounds heal more quickly, help build collagen, protect you from sun damage and free radicals, and reduce wrinkles.

YOUR WAISTLINE. People who eat more minimally processed foods, such as beans, fruits, nuts and seeds, vegetables, and whole grains, and avoid all animal products tend to have a lower weight and body mass index (BMI).

YOUR WALLET. Fancy superfoods and plant-based (but processed) specialty foods can make plant-based eating expensive, but meals centered on beans, seasonal fruits and vegetables, and whole grains are inexpensive AND nutritious.

collard greens; and sesame seeds and tahini are all nutritious sources of calcium without the cholesterol and saturated fat found in dairy products. Think you need to eat seafood and fatty fish to get your heart-healthy omega-3 fats? Think again. Chia, flaxseed, and hemp seeds are valuable sources of heart-healthy fats without the dangerous levels of arsenic, lead, and mercury found in many fish and seafood options.

PASS ON PROCESSED FOODS

Here's my position on processed foods: Ideally, you would eat foods that are not processed at all. Minimally processed foods are okay in moderation, however. Stay away from heavily processed foods.

Let's take a closer look at what is and is not considered "processed." Take soy, for example. Edamame, miso, soybeans, and tempeh are all very close to their whole, natural form—meaning there's virtually nothing added or taken away from the soybeans. Minimally processed soy foods include soy milk and tofu, where soybeans have had their beneficial fiber taken away. These types of minimally processed foods are fine to enjoy in moderation. Heavily processed soy products to avoid are foods containing soy protein concentrate, soy protein isolate, or soybean oil. Virtually all of the original soybean has been removed from those foods, along with its health-promoting properties.

We should also look closely at the humble potato. In its whole, natural form, potatoes are a healthy dietary option, contrary to what some low-carb diet gurus might tell you. Potatoes have fiber, minerals, and vitamins. However, it's obvious that deep-fried potato products, like potato chips and French fries, although technically still plant based, aren't an ideal choice when compared to a whole baked potato.

Although processed foods aren't ideal choices, enjoying minimally processed foods like whole-grain breads, whole-grain and bean pastas, and plant-based "milks" are fine in moderation.

WHAT TO DO ABOUT SALT, OIL, AND SUGAR

You'll find that most recipes in this book have very little added salt, oil, and refined sugar. But this book is not strictly a whole-food, plant-based, salt-, oil-, and sugar-free (WFPB SOS-free) cookbook. I firmly believe that if it's not realistic, it's not sustainable, and I want this book to help set you up for long-term success. Although diets high in refined sugar, salt, and oils have been proven to increase your chances of developing a variety of chronic illnesses, I know how hard (or even impossible) it can be to completely avoid these additions.

A strict WFPB SOS-free diet would mean a life without briny olives or that drizzle of extra-virgin olive oil on a bowl of Sun-Dried Tomato and Herb Polenta Cakes (page 26), and Savory Oatmeal Breakfast Cookies with Maple and Sage (page 21) without the maple syrup. For these reasons, you'll still find salt, oil, and sugar (unrefined) used sparingly, thoughtfully, and judiciously throughout this book. Never fear, though; many of the recipes that use SOS often offer an SOS-free tip to help eliminate those ingredients without losing flavor.

Shopping Strategies for Two

Most grocery stores are set up for people shopping to feed a family, so a few unplanned and impulsive purchases can lead to a lot of food in the trash a week later. But planning ahead can set you up for success.

Buy frequently eaten ingredients in larger quantities. Do you eat a lot of frozen spinach and edamame and notice the bigger bag costs 20 percent less per pound? Decide which items you want to stock up on that store well, and buy them in bulk to save money. And buy seasonally for the freshest produce. Find a Community Supported Agriculture (CSA) farm near you by visiting AMS.USDA .gov/local-food-directories/farmersmarkets.

Buy precut/chopped fruits and vegetables to cut down on food waste, prep time, and leftovers. When planning and preparing meals for two, purchasing a small container of prewashed and cut ingredients means less food will end up in the trash next week and you won't have to eat butternut squash soup eight days in a row.

Purchase frozen fruits and vegetables. Yes, fresh produce may be ideal for salads and sandwiches, but you really can't beat the convenience of frozen vegetables. Buying frozen veggies gives you the option to use only the amount you need and store the rest without worrying about spoilage.

Shop from the bulk bins. Have a recipe that uses a handful of hemp seeds, or want to try a new ancient grain before buying a larger package? Shopping from the bins means you buy only what you need, and that can translate to a smaller grocery bill and less waste.

Stick mostly to the perimeter of the store. That's where you'll find the fruits, veggies, and other fresh foods (where you have more control over the quantities you purchase). Processed foods tend to be in those middle aisles; they're shelf stable and full of added salt and preservatives.

Plant-Based Flavor Boosts

A whole-food, plant-based diet can absolutely contain the comforting flavors and textures you derive from other types of favorite dishes. Here are just a few ingredients that boost flavor in a way that's healthy and delicious.

DATES. Dates are a wholesome fiber- and mineral-packed option for adding sweetness to a dish without adding empty calories. Dates can be used in their whole form, dried and pulverized into "date sugar," or blended with water to form a paste or syrup.

FRESH HERBS AND AROMATICS. When cutting back on salt, oil, and sugar, garlic and onions are your plant-based friends for bumping up the flavor and excitement in savory dishes. Fresh herbs such as basil, cilantro, and mint can boost flavor without adding empty calories. I recommend fresh herbs over their dried counterparts, which lose much of their flavor after just six months of being in the pantry.

MISO. This fermented soybean paste is an umami flavor bomb, and is, by far, my favorite way to add a savory, salty flavor to a dish without adding refined salt. You'll typically find it labeled as "white" or "red/brown," depending on how long it's been aged. White miso is younger and, typically, milder in flavor and tastes a lot like Parmesan cheese, while red miso has a deeper, more developed flavor, like soy sauce. It's an important ingredient in my Mushroom, Lentil, and Spinach Stew (page 51) and the foundation for my Quick Umami Broth (page 110).

NUTRITIONAL YEAST. This is my go-to for adding cheesy flavor without the cholesterol and saturated fat of dairy products. Nutritional yeast is a tasty source of antioxidants, minerals, protein, and vitamins and is a plant-based kitchen staple.

NUTS AND SEEDS. Even without dairy, you can still eat rich and creamy foods. Nuts and seeds have heart-healthy fats, zero cholesterol, and tons of important minerals your body needs, like calcium, magnesium, and zinc. My versatile Savory Nut and Seed Cream Sauce (page 117) makes a delicious and deceptively rich chowder without the need for heavy cream, and blending cashews with vegetables creates the base for my rich and creamy Cheesy Sauce (page 112).

VEGETABLE BROTH. Why cook grains in plain water when you can use broth that can add flavor to your food (see Versatile Vegetable Rice Pilaf, page 37)? When looking to reduce the amount of oil in the pan, using a splash or two of a flavorful broth to stop food from sticking can boost your dish's flavor.

Planning Perfectly Portioned Meals

Planning and prepping your meals and snacks ahead gives you the best chance of success when transitioning to a new way of eating and will help you turn the healthy choice into the easy choice.

Batch-cook whole grains to use throughout the week and beyond. Setting aside 60 minutes once a week to cook a large batch of barley, farro, quinoa, rice, or wheat berries can pay off all week long. My Versatile Vegetable Rice Pilaf (page 37) is ideal to make in double (or triple!) batches and can even be cooked days in advance, then portioned and frozen.

Beans are your planning friend. You'll notice that a lot of recipes in this book center on a single can of beans. Not only are canned beans the fastest and most convenient way to get a plant-based, protein-packed snack or meal on the table, but they're also perfectly portioned for a meal for two. Choose no-salt-added beans in BPA-free cans or Tetra Paks, if you can find them; if you can't, just drain and rinse the beans thoroughly to remove the added salt.

Plan your meals to reuse fresh and perishable ingredients. Delicate fresh herbs such as basil and cilantro are packed with flavor but, unfortunately, don't last very long before they wilt. If you're buying highly perishable foods, plan a few meals with them in the coming days to ensure they do not end up in the trash. Buying a bunch of fresh mint? Plan to make a double batch of my Fruit Magic Dressing (page 113) and my Cucumber and Peach Bellini Fruit Salad (page 29) to use it up before it wilts.

Portion foods once you bring them home. Want to stock up with big savings from your favorite warehouse store and think that a mega-family-size box of brown rice is a great deal? Studies have proven that the bigger the original box of food you buy, the bigger your portion sizes become. Portioning the larger packages of food into smaller, meal-for-two-size containers can translate to more sensible portions at dinnertime.

Set aside time each week to plan and prep. Studies have shown that most people make about 200 food-related decisions each day. Decision fatigue is REAL and can mean the difference between a successful week of healthy meals and a week of takeout, shopping trips, and wasted food.

Your Plant-Based Kitchen for Two

If you're new to cooking or eating plant-based meals, setting up your kitchen and knowing which ingredients to buy can feel a bit intimidating. So, let's dive into what you'll need, want, and love to have in your plant-based kitchen for two.

PANTRY AND COUNTER

Canned tomatoes. You might think fresh tomatoes from the produce section are the best bet, but for most of the year, canned is the go-to for ripe, flavorful tomatoes. They're picked at their peak of flavor and canned within hours, locking in their summer sun-ripened flavors for you to use year-round.

Dried and canned beans. Yes, precooked canned beans are fast and convenient in a pinch, but you just can't beat the price or shelf life of dried beans. Keep both varieties on hand, and you'll always have a quick, reliable, and steady supply of plant-based protein.

Dried whole grains. Barley, brown rice, buckwheat, bulgur, millet, oats, and popcorn are great, long-lasting options to keep in the pantry. Purchasing precooked, two-serving packets of brown rice or other parcooked grains is a good shopping option, but be sure to read the label for added sodium, oil, and preservatives.

Onions and garlic. Store onions and garlic at room temperature in a dry, well-ventilated area for several weeks.

Potatoes and sweet potatoes. Most potato varieties can be stored in a cool, dark, dry pantry or cupboard for several weeks.

Small amounts of nuts and seeds. These include chia seeds, flaxseed, hemp seeds, pumpkin seeds, and sunflower seeds, as well as almonds, peanuts, pecans, and walnuts. The fats in nuts and seeds can spoil quickly—especially in warmer climates. Keep a couple weeks' supply of these nutritional powerhouses close by and store the rest in the freezer.

Spice blends. Don't have the room or budget for an endless array of exotic spices you'll use once a year? Spice blends, like curry powders or salt-free all-purpose seasonings, are the fast and less costly answer to adding big flavor to meals.

Vinegars. Apple cider vinegar, unseasoned rice vinegar, sherry vinegar, and red and white wine vinegars are great for livening up dishes without salt and give a punch of flavor in a pinch.

Whole-grain and bean pastas. You can't beat the shelf life, ease, and versatility of dried pastas. Choose 100-percent whole-grain pastas to ensure you're not missing out on the extra fiber, nutrients, and protein they offer. Need to keep your meals gluten-free? There are now pastas made from chickpeas, lentils, and even edamame.

FRIDGE AND FREEZER

Citrus. Keep lemons and limes in a bowl of fresh water in your fridge and they'll stay fresh for 2 to 3 months.

Fresh herbs. Treat most fresh herbs, such as cilantro, mint, and parsley, as you would cut flowers, but in a glass of water in the fridge. Change the water every few days, and the herbs will last for a couple of weeks. (Exception: basil. This tender herb will blacken and wilt in the fridge. Keep it in water on your counter-top or a sunny windowsill and pick from it as needed all week long.)

Frozen fruits and vegetables. Frozen fruits and vegetables are picked and frozen at their peak of freshness, so stock up on the frozen versions of any produce that spoils quickly, such as strawberries and green leafy veggies. That way, you won't be caught off guard at dinnertime by a wilted bunch of kale.

Green leafy vegetables. Try arugula, kale, lettuces, spinach, and Swiss chard, to name a few. Consider picking up bags of chopped prewashed greens if you're short on time and need to get dinner on the table in a flash. Or, store the greens, washed and ready to go, with a paper towel in the bag or container to absorb moisture and keep them fresher longer.

Larger packages of nuts and seeds. Store large packages of nuts and seeds in the freezer to stop them from going rancid quickly.

Tofu, tempeh, and miso. These minimally processed soybean products can last weeks unopened in the fridge.

Whole-grain breads and tortillas. Store these in the freezer or refrigerator if you're not using them within 3 to 5 days. Whole-grain minimally processed foods like these can go moldy quickly if you're choosing wholesome options without a lot of salt and preservatives.

KITCHEN EQUIPMENT

1-, 2-, and 4-quart nonstick saucepans. Nonstick cookware is essential when cutting back on added oil while cooking. Skip the large stockpots and opt for smaller pots and pans, more useful when cooking for two.

4- to 8-cup oven-safe baking dishes or Dutch ovens. Sure, large casserole dishes are great when serving a crowd, but don't really come in handy when cooking for two.

10-inch nonstick skillet. Perfect for sautéing and quickly cooking a variety of foods on the stovetop. Choose skillets that are nontoxic (PFOA-free or Teflon-free), whenever possible and oven-safe for added versatility.

Baking sheets. Have a few of these at the ready for roasting vegetables.

Blender. You'll find that a lot of recipes in this book use a blender. It can help you whip up a salad dressing, sauce, smoothie, or soup in a matter of minutes. A food processor will work in place of a blender for most recipes.

Chef's knife. A sharp knife in the right hands is one of the most valuable and versatile tools in your kitchen. Find a knife that fits your hand and your budget, and make sure to keep it sharp.

Flexible cutting board(s). Eating more fruits and vegetables means more cutting and prepping. Flexible cutting boards made from BPA-free plastic make transferring cut veggies to a pot or bowl faster and easier.

Immersion stick blender, potato masher, or mini personal blender. Cooking meals for two means smaller volumes of dressings and sauces, perfect for a smaller blender.

Level-up your container game. Having the right storage containers for the pantry, fridge, and freezer can make it easier to portion foods and store them safely until you're ready to cook. Get your hands on 1-, 2-, and 4-cup containers to skip an extra measuring step when portioning foods or leftovers.

Microplane. This tool is necessary for finely mincing flavorful aromatics such as ginger and garlic, as well as zesting citrus.

Silicone baking mats and/or parchment paper. If you're roasting vegetables with less oil, these tools are a must. Reusable silicone mats are an eco-friendly option, whereas parchment paper can be handy to make "packets" for steaming veggies in the oven.

About the Recipes

All of the recipes in this book have been carefully selected and customized to serve two people. I hope you enjoy cooking, eating, and sharing them as much as I enjoyed creating them for you.

RECIPE LABELS

In addition to the nutritional information at the bottom of each recipe, keep your eye out for these specific recipe labels included at the top of each recipe.

5-Ingredient: These recipes have 5 ingredients or fewer, not including oil, salt, pepper, and water.

Gluten-Free: These recipes do not contain barley, rye, wheat, or other gluten-containing ingredients.

One Pot: These recipes are prepped and cooked in one vessel.

SOS-Free and SOS-Free Option: This one requires a bit of explanation. The recipes with an SOS-Free label contain no added salt, oil, or refined sugar. Those with the SOS-Free Option label have only optional salt, oil, or refined sugar in the ingredients list that can be eliminated without affecting the final result negatively. Many of the recipes without the label, though, will have SOS-free tips (see following), so you can make the meal SOS-free.

> **Salt:** For the most part, as a recipe ingredient, miso is used in place of plain old salt, but I do recommend seasoning lightly with sea salt to taste in many recipes. These recipes will not receive the SOS-Free label, although you can feel free to eliminate the salt, if you prefer.

> **Oil:** This one is straightforward. If there is any oil required in a recipe, that recipe will not have the SOS-Free label.

> **Sugar:** As for sugar, there are some acceptable SOS-free sweeteners, such as dates, date sugar, date syrup, whole blended fruit, unsweetened apple sauce, and small amounts of fruit juice (like lemon juice). Recipes with these ingredients earn the SOS-Free label. Recipes with other sweeteners, such as maple syrup, will not have an SOS-Free label because they contain a refined sweetener.

Quick: These recipes take 30 minutes or fewer from prep to table.

RECIPE HELP

After each recipe, you'll also find some helpful suggestions, tips, and tricks.

Cooking tip: These tips offer special guidance regarding ingredients, prepping, or cooking.

SOS-free tip: For many of the recipes that do have a little oil, refined sugar, and/or salt, you'll see suggestions for how you can still make the dish without these ingredients.

Use it again: To avoid waste, these tips suggest other recipes in the book that use the same ingredients.

Variation tip: These tips provide suggestions for swapping out certain ingredients or dialing up the spiciness to suit your personal taste.

Sun-Dried Tomato and Herb Polenta Cakes 26

Chapter Two

BREAKFAST AND BRUNCH

SPICED CHICKPEA GRANOLA

SERVES 2 | **PREP TIME** 10 minutes | **COOK TIME** 25 minutes

Granola off the shelf can be a sugary, oily affair, packed with nutrient-free filler. This unique and flexible granola recipe transforms a simple can of chickpeas into a hearty, nutritious, make-ahead breakfast for two. Feel free to get creative and swap ingredients to match what you like and what is in your pantry.

1 teaspoon olive oil (optional)

1 teaspoon white miso, divided

1 (15-ounce) can no-salt-added chickpeas, drained, aquafaba reserved

½ teaspoon ground cinnamon

¼ teaspoon ground nutmeg

1 tablespoon date syrup (see Cooking tip)

1 tablespoon sunflower seed butter

2 tablespoons pumpkin seeds

2 tablespoons chopped pecans

2 tablespoons sunflower seeds

1. Preheat the oven to 400°F. Line a baking sheet with parchment paper or a silicone baking mat.

2. In a medium mixing bowl, whisk the olive oil (if using), ½ teaspoon of miso, and 2 tablespoons of aquafaba to blend. Toss the chickpeas in the mixture to coat thoroughly and transfer them to the prepared baking sheet.

3. Roast the chickpeas for 10 to 15 minutes, until thoroughly dried but not browned.

4. While the chickpeas roast, in the same mixing bowl, combine the remaining miso, cinnamon, nutmeg, date syrup, and sunflower seed butter and set aside.

5. Remove the chickpeas from the oven (keep the oven on), transfer them to the bowl, and toss to coat. Add the pumpkin seeds, pecans, and sunflower seeds to the bowl and gently stir to coat thoroughly. Transfer the mixture back to the baking sheet.

6. Roast for 10 minutes, until toasted, gently shaking the pan and rotating halfway through. Let the granola cool to room temperature.

7. Refrigerate in an airtight container for up to 1 week.

COOKING TIP: If you have a tough time finding date syrup in the grocery store, make your own: In a blender, combine 4 ounces of dates and 1 cup of water and blend until smooth.

VARIATION TIP: Do you have a sweet tooth? Jazz up this granola with a small handful of dark chocolate chips (once the granola has cooled) or add a handful of dried fruit, like dried blueberries or raisins.

PER SERVING (1 CUP): Calories: 428; Fat: 22g; Sodium: 140mg; Carbohydrates: 46g; Fiber: 13g; Sugar: 14g; Protein: 17g

TOFU SCRAMBLE WITH WILTED GREENS

SERVES 2 | **PREP TIME** 15 minutes | **COOK TIME** 25 minutes

This protein-packed breakfast is as versatile as it is delicious. So, you won't miss the eggs or cheese (or the dietary downsides they bring). This recipe uses a bit of black salt, also known as kala namak, which is known for its egglike flavor. Black salt can be found commonly in Indian grocery stores.

1 teaspoon neutral cooking oil (like vegetable or sunflower seed oil; optional)

1 large garlic clove, minced

1 medium yellow or white onion, diced

2 teaspoons white miso

1/2 teaspoon ground turmeric

1/2 teaspoon dried Italian seasoning

Freshly ground black pepper

1 (14-ounce) block firm tofu, drained and crumbled

2 cups packed fresh baby spinach, kale, or Swiss chard

1 tablespoon nutritional yeast

1/4 teaspoon black salt (see SOS-free tip)

1. Heat a large dry nonstick skillet over low heat for 5 minutes.

2. Pour in the oil (if using). Add the garlic, onion, miso, turmeric, Italian seasoning, and pepper to taste and sauté for 3 to 4 minutes, until the onion has softened and becomes translucent and lightly browned.

3. Add the tofu to the skillet, raise the heat to medium, and cook for about 10 minutes, stirring occasionally to prevent sticking, until the remaining water evaporates and the tofu is lightly browned.

4. Add the spinach to the skillet and stir to incorporate. Cook for 5 minutes so the spinach wilts. Stir in the nutritional yeast, black salt, and season with more pepper to taste. Serve immediately.

SOS-FREE TIP: Skip the salt and add some thinly shaved Brussels sprouts for that eggy flavor. If you're not missing that eggy flavor, swap the salt for equal parts garlic and onion powder. Want to avoid the oil but worried about sticking? Add a few splashes of no-salt-added vegetable broth to the pan.

PER SERVING (1 1/2 CUPS): Calories: 246; Fat: 10g; Sodium: 417mg; Carbohydrates: 16g; Fiber: 5g; Sugar: 5g; Protein: 24g

CINNAMON-APPLE HUMMUS

SERVES 2 | **PREP TIME** 10 minutes

Who says hummus is only a savory dip for a vegetable platter? Not me! Kick that butter and cream cheese to the curb, and slather this sweet-tasting, sweet-smelling spread on apple slices or whole-grain bread for a protein-, fiber-, and flavor-filled breakfast on the go.

1 (15-ounce) can no-salt-added chickpeas, drained and rinsed

1 teaspoon white miso

2 Medjool dates, pitted and chopped

½ cup unsweetened applesauce

2 tablespoons sunflower seed butter

½ teaspoon ground cinnamon

In a medium mixing bowl, combine the chickpeas, miso, dates, applesauce, sunflower seed butter, and cinnamon. Using a potato masher, thoroughly mash all the ingredients to achieve a rustic, spreadable texture. Refrigerate in an airtight container for up to 5 days.

VARIATION TIP: Stir in some chopped walnuts or dried fruit, like raisins, to add more texture.

PER SERVING (¾ CUP): Calories: 366; Fat: 13g; Sodium: 165mg; Carbohydrates: 50g; Fiber: 14g; Sugar: 18g; Protein: 14g

PIÑA COLADA QUINOA PORRIDGE

SERVES 2 | **PREP TIME** 5 minutes | **COOK TIME** 30 minutes

Quinoa, a South American gluten-free grain, has gained tremendous popularity for its high protein content and nutty flavor. This complete protein also offers antioxidants, fiber, and a plethora of essential vitamins and minerals. For this reason, quinoa is considered a "superfood" and makes a perfect replacement for more traditional breakfast grains, like oats or grits. It gets a taste of the tropics here.

1¼ cups water

2 Medjool dates, pitted

1 teaspoon white miso

1 tablespoon coconut butter

½ cup quinoa, rinsed (see tip)

1 cup frozen and thawed or fresh pineapple chunks

¼ cup shredded unsweetened coconut (optional)

1. In a blender, combine the water, dates, miso, and coconut butter and blend until smooth.

2. Heat a medium dry nonstick saucepan over low heat for 5 minutes.

3. Pour in the quinoa and cook for 3 minutes, stirring constantly, until it is lightly toasted.

4. Stir the coconut butter mixture into the quinoa, turn the heat to high, and bring it to a rolling boil. Reduce the heat to low and gently simmer for about 20 minutes, stirring occasionally, or until the quinoa is cooked and has a creamy porridge consistency.

5. Remove from the heat and stir in the pineapple and coconut (if using). Serve this dish warm or chilled.

COOKING TIP: Quinoa has a naturally occurring, and slightly bitter, soaplike coating called saponin. Most store-bought quinoas are unrinsed, so you may want to purchase pre-rinsed quinoa or rinse the quinoa several times in a colander under running water to remove this bitter coating before adding it to the pot.

PER SERVING (1 CUP): Calories: 281; Fat: 8g; Sodium: 99mg; Carbohydrates: 49g; Fiber: 7g; Sugar: 18g; Protein: 7g

SAVORY OATMEAL BREAKFAST COOKIES WITH MAPLE AND SAGE

SERVES 2 | **PREP TIME** 20 minutes | **COOK TIME** 40 minutes

Eating a plant-based diet does not mean you have to miss the foods and flavors you love. This unique breakfast cookie recipe is reminiscent of your favorite maple and sage breakfast sausage, but without the cholesterol-raising properties and saturated fat. And who wouldn't want a guilt-free cookie for breakfast?

1 cup Quick Umami Broth (page 110), or store-bought low-sodium vegetable broth

1 teaspoon olive oil

2 teaspoons maple syrup

1 teaspoon dried sage

1 tablespoon Italian seasoning

½ teaspoon garlic powder

½ teaspoon onion powder

⅛ teaspoon cayenne pepper

½ teaspoon sea salt (optional)

1 cup old-fashioned rolled oats

1. Preheat the oven to 375°F. Line a baking sheet with parchment paper or a silicone baking mat.

2. In a medium nonstick saucepan, combine the broth, oil, maple syrup, sage, Italian seasoning, garlic powder, onion powder, cayenne, and salt (if using) and bring to a boil over medium-high heat.

3. Remove the pan from the heat, stir in the oats, and allow the cookie mixture to sit for 10 minutes to cool and fully absorb the liquid.

4. Divide the mixture in half and gently flatten each portion into a round cookie. Place the cookies on the prepared baking sheet.

5. Bake for 15 minutes, flip the cookies over, and bake for 15 minutes more. Let the cookies cool.

6. Refrigerate in an airtight container for up to 5 days.

COOKING TIP: Make these the night before and toast them in a toaster oven or microwave for 20 seconds for a warm breakfast cookie on the go.

PER SERVING (1 COOKIE): Calories: 207; Fat: 6g; Sodium: 88mg; Carbohydrates: 36g; Fiber: 5g; Sugar: 6g; Protein: 6g

CHICKPEA FRITTATA WITH SEASONAL VEGETABLES

SERVES 2 | **PREP TIME** 15 minutes | **COOK TIME** 40 minutes

This eggless chickpea frittata is filling, easy, delicious, and creative way to use up leftover roasted vegetables. The batter can even be used to make pancakes, crêpes, or a crustless quiche. Get creative with the ingredients and adjust the number and types of vegetables and herbs to suit your tastes.

2/3 cup chickpea flour

2/3 cup water

2 tablespoons sunflower seed butter

2 teaspoons white miso

1 teaspoon dried Italian seasoning

1 teaspoon olive oil (optional)

1/8 teaspoon black salt (optional; see tip)

1/8 teaspoon ground turmeric

1/8 teaspoon red pepper flakes

1 1/2 cups finely chopped mixed seasonal vegetables and herbs:

Winter: Brussels sprouts, kale, leeks, parsley

Spring: Asparagus, chives, fennel, green peas

Summer: Basil, eggplant, red bell pepper, zucchini

Autumn: Beets, carrots, parsnips, rosemary

1. Preheat the oven to 375°F.

2. In a medium mixing bowl, whisk the flour, water, sunflower seed butter, miso, Italian seasoning, oil (if using), black salt (if using), turmeric, and red pepper flakes until smooth.

3. Add the seasonal vegetables and herbs to the batter and gently stir to combine thoroughly. Pour the mixture into a small 4-cup nonstick baking dish.

4. Bake for 35 to 40 minutes, until the top is slightly cracked and golden brown or until a toothpick inserted into the middle comes out clean.

VARIATION TIP: Don't have or want to use black salt? Add 1/2 teaspoon of garlic powder and 1/4 teaspoon of onion powder or 1 garlic clove, minced, to the batter.

PER SERVING (1/2 FRITTATA): Calories: 300; Fat: 12g; Sodium: 267mg; Carbohydrates: 36g; Fiber: 12g; Sugar: 7g; Protein: 15g

BLUEBERRY AND MINT POWER SMOOTHIE

SERVES 2 | **PREP TIME** 5 minutes

Smoothies came into being around the time blenders were invented in the 1930s. Their popularity grew as healthy foods became more popular in the 1970s. This subtly sweet smoothie is packed with antioxidants, fiber, heart-healthy fats, and enough protein to keep you feeling energized and satisfied throughout your busy morning.

1½ cups frozen blueberries

1 medium banana, peeled

2 cups lightly packed chopped curly kale

¼ cup hemp seeds

1 cup no-salt-added cannellini beans, drained and rinsed

¼ cup lightly packed fresh mint leaves, chopped

2 cups water

In a blender, combine the blueberries, banana, kale, hemp seeds, beans, mint, and water. Blend on high speed for 1 minute, or until smooth.

COOKING TIP: Prep, measure, and place all the ingredients, except the water, in a freezer bag the night before to turn this into a 2-minute grab-and-go breakfast.

PER SERVING (3 CUPS): Calories: 386; Fat: 12g; Sodium: 56mg; Carbohydrates: 55g; Fiber: 14g; Sugar: 24g; Protein: 15g

LEMON AND DILL BROILED TOFU

SERVES 2 | **PREP TIME** 10 minutes, plus 15 minutes to marinate
COOK TIME 10 minutes

Before going plant based, eggs Benedict with hollandaise sauce was my brunch jam. This dish completely satisfies that craving, using a variation of my Cheesy Sauce (page 112) with lots of fresh lemon and dill that will make you forget all about old Benedict what's-his-name and quickly become your new plant-based, heart-thanking-you, brunch best friend.

2 garlic cloves, finely minced

4 tablespoons freshly squeezed lemon juice, divided

Grated zest of 2 lemons, divided

1 tablespoon olive oil

2 teaspoons white miso

1/8 teaspoon freshly ground black pepper

1/2 (14-ounce) package extra-firm tofu, drained, pressed, and cut into 1-inch-thick steaks

1 cup Cheesy Sauce (page 112)

1/4 cup chopped fresh dill

1. In a small bowl, whisk the garlic, 2 tablespoons of lemon juice, the zest of 1 lemon, oil, miso, and pepper to blend. Place the tofu steaks in a shallow baking dish and pour the marinade over the tofu, ensuring it is coated thoroughly. Refrigerate for at least 15 minutes, so the tofu can absorb the marinade.

2. While the tofu marinates, in a small saucepan over medium heat, heat the cheesy sauce until hot. Whisk in the remaining 2 tablespoons of lemon juice, remaining zest of 1 lemon, and the dill. Keep warm over low heat until ready to serve.

3. Just before mealtime, preheat the broiler to high.

4. Broil the marinated tofu for 3 to 4 minutes per side, until heated through and slightly browned. Serve the broiled tofu steaks with the cheesy lemon-dill sauce.

COOKING TIP: Make the marinade the night before and marinate the tofu overnight in the fridge for full flavor.

PER SERVING (1 "STEAK" AND 1/2 CUP SAUCE): Calories: 254; Fat: 14g; Sodium: 268mg; Carbohydrates: 18g; Fiber: 5g; Sugar: 4g; Protein: 16g

HONEYDEW AND ROASTED POBLANO FRUIT SALAD

SERVES 2 | **PREP TIME** 10 minutes | **COOK TIME** 20 minutes, plus 10 minutes to rest

We've all seen it—an uninspired bowl of fruit salad remaining on the brunch table, long after all the other tasty trays have been emptied. No more. Make just the right amount and take your fruit to the next level with my Fruit Magic Dressing (page 113), some mildly spicy poblano peppers, and fresh mint. You'll see; it'll disappear from your table like magic.

2 poblano peppers

3 cups cubed (1 inch) honeydew melon

2 tablespoons finely chopped fresh mint leaves

½ cup Fruit Magic Dressing (page 113)

1. Preheat the broiler.

2. Place the poblanos on a baking sheet and broil the peppers for 3 minutes per side, or until the skin is blistered and blackened. Place the broiled peppers in a heatproof bowl and cover. Let steam for 5 minutes. When cool enough to handle, remove the skin and seeds before chopping the peppers and placing them in a medium mixing bowl.

3. Stir in the honeydew, mint, and dressing to combine with the peppers and let sit for 5 to 10 minutes, so the flavors combine before serving.

COOKING TIP: Having a tough time finding fresh mint leaves at your local grocery store? Head to the coffee and tea aisle instead and buy some peppermint tea. Add ¼ teaspoon of dried peppermint tea to the Fruit Magic Dressing before tossing with the salad.

PER SERVING (1½ CUPS): Calories: 320; Fat: 17g; Sodium: 269mg; Carbohydrates: 42g; Fiber: 8g; Sugar: 28g; Protein: 9g

SUN-DRIED TOMATO AND HERB POLENTA CAKES

SERVES 2 | **PREP TIME** 5 minutes, plus overnight to chill (optional)
COOK TIME 40 minutes

This recipe can be prepared two ways: You can cook the polenta a day in advance and allow it to cool and solidify into "cakes" in the fridge overnight. With that option, you will grill or sauté the polenta just before serving. A second option is to serve it immediately, when it still has a soft grits-like consistency. Either way, it is a flavorful savory dish. Plus, polenta contains both fiber and protein, so it is also a nutritious and filling option.

⅛ teaspoon red pepper flakes

1 small garlic clove, minced

1 teaspoon white miso

1 teaspoon dried Italian seasoning

2 tablespoons nutritional yeast

4 sun-dried tomato halves, chopped

1 cup water

Freshly ground black pepper

½ cup polenta

2 teaspoons olive oil, divided

1 cup Easy Marinara Sauce (page 114), or store-bought low-sodium marinara, warmed

1. In a medium saucepan, combine the red pepper flakes, garlic, miso, Italian seasoning, nutritional yeast, sun-dried tomatoes, water, and black pepper to taste. Place the pan over medium-high heat and bring to a boil. Whisk in the polenta and let the mixture return to a boil. Reduce the heat to medium-low and gently simmer for about 30 minutes, or until the polenta is very thick.

2. Pour the polenta into a 4-cup baking dish and spread it into an even layer. Either (a) serve immediately; or (b) cover and let the polenta cool overnight in the fridge.

3. If you opted for (b), once the polenta has solidified in the fridge, turn out the "cake" onto a cutting board and cut it into two equal portions. Heat a nonstick skillet over medium-high heat for 5 minutes. Brush both sides of each polenta cake with 1 teaspoon of oil and place it in the hot skillet. Cook for 3 to 4 minutes per side, flipping only once to avoid the cake breaking, until golden brown.

4. Serve the polenta topped with the warmed marinara and drizzle the remaining 1 teaspoon of oil over top.

COOKING TIP: Reduce your cooking time significantly by choosing "quick-cooking" or instant polenta. Just be sure to adjust the polenta-to-water ratio according to the package instructions. When choosing sun-dried tomatoes, look for those that are packed dry; oil-packed tomatoes in jars are fine, too, if you can't find dry packed.

PER SERVING (1 CAKE OR 1/2 CUP SOFT POLENTA WITH 1/2 CUP SAUCE): Calories: 257; Fat: 7g; Sodium: 112mg; Carbohydrates: 40g; Fiber: 7g; Sugar: 5g; Protein: 10g

CARAMEL LATTE OVERNIGHT OATS

SERVES 2 | **PREP TIME** 20 minutes, plus overnight to chill

This recipe elevates plain old overnight oats to new heights. If you like your coffee with extra cream and sugar, then this is the recipe for you. You can even serve it in a mug, although you'll be having your morning fave in more of a parfait style, rather than as a drink. Add a dollop of plant-based yogurt, another spoonful of almond butter, or a couple more dates to the blender to suit your tastes, or top with chopped almonds or chocolate chips.

1½ cups strong brewed coffee

4 Medjool dates, pitted and chopped

2 tablespoons smooth almond butter

¼ teaspoon vanilla bean powder, or ½ teaspoon vanilla extract

1 cup old-fashioned rolled oats

1. In a blender, combine the coffee, dates, almond butter, and vanilla and blend until smooth.

2. In a small mixing bowl, combine the coffee mixture and oats, stirring thoroughly to mix. Divide the mixture between two airtight containers and refrigerate overnight.

COOKING TIP: Do not choose quick or instant oats for this recipe, as they break down quickly in liquid and will turn your oatmeal into a slimy mush.

PER SERVING (ABOUT ¾ CUP): Calories: 293; Fat: 12g; Sodium: 3mg; Carbohydrates: 41g; Fiber: 7g; Sugar: 11g; Protein: 9g

CUCUMBER AND PEACH BELLINI FRUIT SALAD

SERVES 2 | **PREP TIME** 10 minutes | **COOK TIME** 25 minutes

I found inspiration for this dish in one of my favorite brunch cocktails: the Bellini, an Italian cocktail similar to the French mimosa but with prosecco and peach puree. It may seem strange, at first, to add cucumbers to a fruit salad, but soon you'll be adding them to all your fruit salads for the light, fresh flavor they bring to a dish. I use fiber-rich barley as the grain here for its slightly nutty flavor and chewy texture.

½ cup dried barley

1½ cups water

2 fresh peaches, or
1 cup thawed frozen
peaches, diced

1 large cucumber, peeled,
seeded, and diced

1 tablespoon chopped
fresh mint or basil leaves

½ cup Fruit Magic
Dressing (page 113)

1. In a small saucepan, combine the barley and water and bring to a boil over medium-high heat. Reduce the heat to maintain a simmer and cook for about 20 minutes, until tender.

2. While the barley cooks, in a medium mixing bowl, gently stir together the peaches, cucumber, mint, and dressing and set aside.

3. Drain any remaining water from the barley and place the cooked barley on a clean dish towel or paper towels and let dry thoroughly, about 5 minutes. Once the barley is dry, stir it into the fruit salad and enjoy.

COOKING TIP: This salad is great after it has had a chance to sit overnight in the fridge, as the barley absorbs the dressing. If you choose to make it the night before, wait until just before serving to add the mint or basil to prevent the herb from blackening.

VARIATION TIP: Use brown rice instead of barley to make this recipe gluten-free.

PER SERVING (2 CUPS): Calories: 449; Fat: 18g; Sodium: 224mg; Carbohydrates: 65g; Fiber: 16g; Sugar: 18g; Protein: 15g

Veggie Nacho Platter for Two **34**

Chapter Three

SNACKS AND SIDES

SWEET AND SPICY PECAN BUTTER POPCORN

SERVES 2 | **PREP TIME** 5 minutes | **COOK TIME** 10 minutes

Even though most homemade popcorn recipes call for using a lot of oil, you can actually make popcorn at home without using ANY oil as long as you follow three simple rules: Purchase new popcorn kernels and use them within 1 month of purchase, keep the heat under the pan at medium-low, and shake the pan frequently.

1 tablespoon pecan butter (see Cooking tip)

1 teaspoon white miso

1 teaspoon maple syrup

⅛ teaspoon chili powder

3 tablespoons fresh popcorn kernels

Sea salt (optional)

1. In a small bowl, whisk the pecan butter, miso, maple syrup, and chili powder to blend. Set aside.

2. Heat a medium nonstick saucepan with a tight-fitting lid over medium-low heat for 5 minutes.

3. Add the kernels to the pan, cover the pan tightly, and shake the pan every few seconds to prevent the popcorn from burning and sticking. The kernels will begin popping in 1 to 2 minutes.

4. Cook, shaking the pot, until the sound of popping kernels slows to every 3 to 5 seconds; remove from the heat.

5. Thin the consistency of the pecan butter drizzle with 1 tablespoon of water, if needed, and drizzle it over the popcorn. Season with salt (if using) to taste.

COOKING TIP: Swap pecan butter for another nut or seed butter (but not peanut butter) in its place. Choose one with a consistency that can be drizzled.

VARIATION TIP: Swap the chili powder for smoked paprika for a sweet and smoky flavor.

PER SERVING (2 CUPS): Calories: 134; Fat: 7g; Sodium: 95mg; Carbohydrates: 19g; Fiber: 4g; Sugar: 3g; Protein: 3g

ROASTED GREEN PEAS WITH LEMON AND MINT

SERVES 2 | **PREP TIME** 5 minutes | **COOK TIME** 20 minutes

Move over roasted chickpeas, there's another crunchy, protein-packed snack in town. Low in sugar and high in vitamin C and fiber, peas can hold their own as the center of this side dish or appetizer. Using a bag of frozen peas means this recipe comes together in minutes.

1 (10-ounce) bag frozen green peas, thawed

2 teaspoons white miso

1 tablespoon tahini

2 tablespoons freshly squeezed lemon juice

1 teaspoon grated lemon zest (optional)

1 tablespoon finely chopped fresh mint leaves

1. Preheat the oven to 400°F. Line a baking sheet with parchment paper or a silicone baking mat.

2. Place the thawed peas on a dry, clean kitchen towel or paper towels to let the excess moisture drain.

3. In a medium mixing bowl, whisk the miso, tahini, and lemon juice to blend. Toss in the peas and gently mix to coat thoroughly. Transfer the peas to the prepared baking sheet.

4. Roast for about 20 minutes, shaking and rotating the sheet pan after 10 minutes, until lightly browned and crunchy.

5. Transfer the peas to a clean, dry bowl and toss with the lemon zest (if using) and mint leaves. Serve immediately, or let the peas cool and transfer them to an airtight container where they will keep at room temperature for up to 1 week.

VARIATION TIP: This recipe is equally delicious if you swap the mint for other fresh herbs, like cilantro or dill.

PER SERVING (½ CUP): Calories: 168; Fat: 5g; Sodium: 342mg; Carbohydrates: 24g; Fiber: 8g; Sugar: 9g; Protein: 10g

VEGGIE NACHO PLATTER FOR TWO

SERVES 2 | **PREP TIME** 15 minutes | **COOK TIME** 25 minutes

This lighter, healthier version of the ubiquitous nacho appetizer will not ruin your appetite for dinner. It's my go-to for game day and is easily customizable with your salsa of choice or other fresh toppings, like corn, pico de gallo, or shredded lettuce.

6 (6-inch) whole-grain organic corn tortillas

2 tablespoons freshly squeezed lime juice

1 cup Cheesy Sauce (page 112)

½ cup 5-Minute Tomato Salsa (page 115) or store-bought, divided

1 cup no-salt-added black beans, drained and rinsed

¼ cup chopped fresh cilantro leaves and stems

¼ cup finely chopped scallions, white and green parts

2 tablespoons thinly sliced jalapeño pepper (optional)

2 limes, cut into wedges

1. Preheat the oven to 400°F. Line a baking sheet with parchment paper or a silicone baking mat.

2. Cut each tortilla into 6 wedges and lightly brush both sides of the tortillas with the lime juice. Place them on the prepared baking sheet, spaced evenly.

3. Bake for 10 minutes, flip the chips, and bake for 10 to 15 minutes more, until crisp and lightly browned.

4. While the tortillas bake, in a small nonstick saucepan over medium heat, combine the cheesy sauce and ¼ cup of salsa and heat until simmering. Keep warm.

5. Arrange the tortillas on a large plate or platter. Just before serving, pour the warm nacho cheese sauce over the chips and top with the black beans, cilantro, scallions, remaining ¼ cup of salsa, and jalapeños (if using). Serve the lime wedges on the side for squeezing.

COOKING TIP: These oil-free tortilla chips can be made in advance and stored in an airtight container at room temperature for up to 5 days. Try them as dipping chips with Lima Bean and Avocado Guacamole (page 35).

PER SERVING (½ RECIPE): Calories: 386; Fat: 5g; Sodium: 124mg; Carbohydrates: 76g; Fiber: 19g; Sugar: 6g; Protein: 16g

LIMA BEAN AND AVOCADO GUACAMOLE

SERVES 2 | **PREP TIME** 10 minutes | **COOK TIME** 15 minutes

Lima beans, grown and eaten for centuries in Central and South America, were often imported to the United States from Peru, which is how they earned their name "lima," after the Peruvian capital. These underrated beans are a surprisingly high-fiber addition to this reduced-fat guacamole recipe. You'll be amazed at how this bean sneaks in under the radar and wins over even the most voracious critic.

3 cups water

1 cup frozen lima beans

1 garlic clove, minced

2 teaspoons white miso

Juice of 1 lime

Grated zest of 1 lime

1 to 2 teaspoons finely chopped red Fresno chile

1 small or ½ large avocado, peeled, pitted, and mashed

½ cup chopped fresh tomato

¼ cup finely chopped scallions, white and green parts

½ cup finely chopped fresh cilantro

1. Fill a large bowl with ice and cold water and set aside.

2. In a medium saucepan, bring the water to a boil. Add the lima beans, lower the heat to medium, and simmer for 7 to 10 minutes, or until tender. Drain the beans and place them in the ice bath to cool and stop the cooking.

3. Drain the cooled beans and place them in a medium bowl. Using the back of a fork or spoon, mash the beans into a smooth paste. Add the garlic, miso, lime juice, lime zest, and chile to taste and stir to combine thoroughly.

4. Just before serving, gently stir in the avocado, tomato, scallions, and cilantro.

VARIATION TIP: Easily dial the heat up or down in this recipe to suit your tastes. Don't have red Fresno chiles? Try a generous pinch of red pepper flakes, a dash or two of your favorite hot sauce, or other chiles, such as jalapeño or habanero, for an extra spicy kick.

PER SERVING (1 CUP): Calories: 255; Fat: 11g; Sodium: 234mg; Carbohydrates: 34g; Fiber: 12g; Sugar: 3g; Protein: 9g

SUMMER BLUEBERRY AND TOMATO SALSA

SERVES 2 | **PREP TIME** 15 minutes

This recipe will bring back beach days, barbecues, and bathing suits. It is best made at the peak of warm summer weather, when tomatoes and berries are at their ripest and most flavorful, but it can also be made year-round using frozen berries. Serve this salsa with your chips of choice or some sliced radishes and cucumbers for a light summer snack.

¼ teaspoon olive oil (optional)

1 teaspoon white miso

1 teaspoon finely minced red Fresno chile or jalapeño pepper

1 tablespoon freshly squeezed lime juice

1 teaspoon grated lime zest

1 cup fresh or frozen blueberries

1 cup chopped tomato

2 scallions, white and green parts, finely chopped

¼ cup finely chopped fresh basil leaves

½ cup diced avocado

1. In a medium mixing bowl, whisk the oil (if using), miso, chile, lime juice, and lime zest to combine. Add the blueberries, tomato, and scallions and toss to coat thoroughly.

2. Just before serving, gently fold in the basil and avocado.

VARIATION TIP: Strawberries, fresh or frozen, are also tasty in this salsa recipe. Don't have fresh basil? Cilantro or mint work well, too.

PER SERVING (1 CUP): Calories: 122; Fat: 5g; Sodium: 98mg; Carbohydrates: 20g; Fiber: 6g; Sugar: 11g; Protein: 3g

VERSATILE VEGETABLE RICE PILAF

SERVES 2 | **PREP TIME** 10 minutes | **COOK TIME** 1 hour

You'll want to make this recipe in double, and even TRIPLE, batches once you discover how versatile and delicious it is. It can be made a few days in advance to be used throughout the week in burritos or nori rolls for a quick weeknight dinner. Or, try it as a base for curry or stir-fry bowls—the options are endless.

½ teaspoon olive oil (optional)

1 teaspoon white miso

½ yellow or white onion, diced

1 cup grated carrots

1 celery stalk, finely diced

1¼ cups Quick Umami Broth (page 110), or store-bought low-sodium vegetable broth

⅓ cup brown rice, rinsed

1 cup frozen peas, thawed

¼ cup finely chopped fresh parsley

1. Heat a medium nonstick saucepan over low heat for 5 minutes.

2. Pour in the oil (if using) and add the miso, onion, carrots, and celery. Cook for 5 to 8 minutes, stirring frequently, until the vegetables have softened and the onion is translucent.

3. Stir in the broth and rice and bring to a boil over medium-high heat. Turn the heat to medium-low, cover the pan, and simmer the rice for 45 minutes.

4. About 5 minutes before the rice is fully cooked, sprinkle the peas on top of the rice in a single layer, replace the lid, and cook for the remaining 5 minutes. DO NOT STIR the peas into the rice.

5. Remove the rice from the heat and gently fold in the parsley, incorporating the peas. Re-cover the pan and let sit for 5 minutes before serving.

COOKING TIP: Stirring the rice when you add the peas will release its starch and make the rice gloopy. If you want fluffy rice, do not stir it while it's cooking.

USE IT AGAIN: Want to use this rice in burrito bowls? Stir in ½ cup of salsa with the broth, or ½ teaspoon of smoked paprika, and swap the peas for frozen corn.

PER SERVING (1 CUP): Calories: 192; Fat: 2g; Sodium: 328mg; Carbohydrates: 40g; Fiber: 8g; Sugar: 9g; Protein: 8g

GARLIC MASHED ROOT VEGETABLES

SERVES 2 | **PREP TIME** 15 minutes | **COOK TIME** 35 minutes

Traditional mashed potato recipes rely on a lot of salt, butter, and heavy cream to boost flavor and give the potatoes a creamy texture. This recipe, on the other hand, uses a variety of vegetables, herbs, aromatics, and heart-healthy fats to make it rich, creamy, and delicious. It makes a delicious side for my Roasted Cauliflower Steak and Mushrooms (page 80).

1/2 cup diced yellow onion

2 teaspoons white miso

2 garlic cloves, minced

1 cup Quick Umami Broth (page 110), or store-bought low-sodium vegetable broth, divided

1 cup diced celery root

1 cup diced white sweet potato or other sweet potato

2 cups diced Yukon Gold potatoes (from 2 or 3 potatoes)

1 cup frozen kale

1/2 cup Savory Nut and Seed Cream Sauce (page 117), or store-bought plant-based Alfredo sauce (like Primal Kitchen)

2 tablespoons nutritional yeast

Sea salt

Freshly ground black pepper

1. Heat a medium nonstick saucepan over low heat for 5 minutes.

2. In the hot pan, combine the onion, miso, and garlic. Cook for 3 to 5 minutes, stirring frequently, until the onion has softened.

3. Stir in the broth, celery root, and sweet potato, and Yukon Gold potatoes. Turn the heat to medium-high and bring the mixture to a boil. Reduce the heat to medium-low and gently simmer for about 15 minutes, or until the vegetables are tender. Stir in the frozen kale and cook for 5 minutes.

4. Remove the pot from the heat and stir in the cream sauce and nutritional yeast. Smash the mixture with a potato masher and season with salt and pepper to taste.

COOKING TIP: The smaller you dice the vegetables, the faster this dish will cook.

PER SERVING (11/2 CUPS): Calories: 443; Fat: 8g; Sodium: 518mg; Carbohydrates: 83g; Fiber: 16g; Sugar: 13g; Protein: 18g

QUICK AND ZESTY CUCUMBERS

SERVES 2 | **PREP TIME** 15 minutes

This recipe is a flavor bomb inspired by a Korean dish called *oi muchim* (which means "seasoned cucumber"). Don't be scared of using more chili powder than you think you should because Korean red chili powder isn't as spicy as some others, like cayenne pepper. You can even add edamame, cooked grains, and salad greens to make this a complete meal in minutes.

1 teaspoon toasted sesame oil

2 teaspoons white miso

1 tablespoon Korean red chili powder (see Variation tip)

1 tablespoon date syrup (see Spiced Chickpea Granola, Cooking tip, page 17)

1 medium garlic clove, minced

1 teaspoon peeled and minced fresh ginger

2 tablespoons unseasoned rice vinegar

2 scallions, white and green parts, finely chopped

1 English cucumber, thinly sliced

1 teaspoon sesame seeds

1. In a medium mixing bowl, whisk the sesame oil, miso, chili powder, date syrup, garlic, ginger, and vinegar to combine. Add the scallions and cucumber to the bowl and toss the vegetables to coat thoroughly.

2. Sprinkle with the sesame seeds and serve immediately.

COOKING TIP: As this dish sits, the cucumbers will continue to release a lot of water, so serve it quickly.

SOS-FREE TIP: Skip the sesame oil. Heat a small nonstick skillet over low heat for 5 minutes. Add 2 tablespoons of sesame seeds and toast for 3 to 5 minutes, stirring frequently, until the seeds are fragrant. This will add the same roasted sesame flavor without the oil.

VARIATION TIP: If you can't find Korean red chili powder, add some fresh Thai chiles (careful of their heat!), gochujang—a fermented Korean chili paste—or green or red Thai curry paste.

PER SERVING (1 CUP): Calories: 117; Fat: 4g; Sodium: 364mg; Carbohydrates: 19g; Fiber: 4g; Sugar: 12g; Protein: 4g

FIRECRACKER GREEN BEANS

SERVES 2 | **PREP TIME** 10 minutes | **COOK TIME** 20 minutes

Green beans, string beans, haricots verts—whatever you call them, these legumes are high in fiber, low in calories, and a rich source of vitamins. Although green beans are often served drowning in an ocean of salty cream of mushroom soup, this recipe is faster, easier, and much more flavorful than your typical green bean casserole. What's not to love about that?

6 cups water

8 ounces string beans, ends trimmed and strings removed

2 teaspoons olive oil

1 medium garlic clove, minced

1 scallion, white and green parts, finely chopped

1 teaspoon sesame seeds

½ teaspoon mustard seeds

¼ teaspoon red pepper flakes

½ teaspoon curry powder

1 tablespoon nutritional yeast

Sea salt

Freshly ground black pepper

1. In a medium nonstick saucepan, bring the water to a rolling boil. Add the beans and cook for 4 to 5 minutes, until just tender but still crisp. Drain the beans and place them on a clean, dry kitchen towel to drain the excess moisture.

2. While the beans dry, heat the same saucepan over medium-low heat for 3 minutes.

3. Pour in the oil and heat until it shimmers. Add the garlic and scallion and cook for about 1 minute, stirring, until softened and aromatic. Add the sesame seeds, mustard seeds, red pepper flakes, and curry powder. Cook for about 3 minutes, stirring to toast and bloom the seeds and spices, or until fragrant.

4. Return the green beans to the saucepan and toss thoroughly to reheat and coat the beans in the spices. Sprinkle with the nutritional yeast and season with salt and pepper to taste.

VARIATION TIP: Get creative and experiment with different spice blends and aromatics. These green beans are also great with some fresh ginger and Chinese five-spice powder instead of the curry powder.

PER SERVING (1 CUP): Calories: 112; Fat: 6g; Sodium: 11mg; Carbohydrates: 11g; Fiber: 5g; Sugar: 4g; Protein: 5g

CREAMY GARLIC SAUTÉED GREENS

SERVES 2 | **PREP TIME** 10 minutes | **COOK TIME** 15 minutes

No more passé creamed spinach here. Give your plain steamed greens a boost in taste and texture with this lighter, easier, updated version of the old creamy dish. Using chickpeas, nuts, and seeds not only elevates the taste, but also the nutritional value.

1 cup no-salt-added chickpeas, drained and rinsed

1 cup Savory Nut and Seed Cream Sauce (page 117), or store-bought plant-based Alfredo sauce (like Primal Kitchen)

2 garlic cloves, minced

6 cups chopped stemmed kale, spinach, or Swiss chard

2 tablespoons freshly squeezed lemon juice

1. In a blender, combine the chickpeas, cream sauce, and garlic and blend until smooth. Transfer the mixture to a 2-quart nonstick saucepan, place it over medium heat, and heat until simmering.

2. Add the chopped greens and cook for about 10 minutes, stirring frequently, until the greens have wilted and are tender. Stir in the lemon juice, and remove from the heat. Serve immediately.

COOKING TIP: If you're short on time, use bags of prewashed, chopped, and ready-to-use greens to turn this into an even quicker side dish you and your plant-based partner will love.

PER SERVING (1 CUP): Calories: 404; Fat: 19g; Sodium: 118mg; Carbohydrates: 47g; Fiber: 16g; Sugar: 6g; Protein: 18g

Vegetable Stew with Dumplings 54

Chapter Four

SOUPS AND STEWS

ZESTY TOMATO GAZPACHO

SERVES 2 | **PREP TIME** 20 minutes

Soup isn't just for those cold, cozy winter evenings. This chilled tomato soup takes advantage of ripe summer fruits at their peak of flavor, comes together in a matter of minutes, and is even better if it's had a day or two to chill out in the fridge. I keep a small pitcher of this in my refrigerator all summer long and it's my go-to for a refreshing lunch.

1 pound Roma or plum tomatoes, cored and coarsely chopped

1 small cucumber, peeled and chopped

1 medium garlic clove, chopped

½ red bell pepper, chopped

1½ tablespoons sherry vinegar or red wine vinegar

1 tablespoon white miso

1 teaspoon olive oil

2 scallions, white and green parts, diced

1 cup no-salt-added chickpeas, drained and rinsed

½ cup halved cherry tomatoes

¼ cup finely chopped fresh basil leaves

In a blender, combine the Roma tomatoes, cucumber, garlic, bell pepper, vinegar, miso, and oil and blend until smooth. Transfer to an airtight container and stir in the scallions, chickpeas, cherry tomatoes, and basil. Cover and refrigerate until you're ready to serve, or for up to 1 week where it will continue to develop flavor as it sits.

COOKING TIP: Adjust the seasonings in this recipe depending on how flavorful your tomatoes are. When tomatoes are at their best, go easy on the seasoning and allow them to shine. But when they're less than ideal, bump up the flavor with some more miso, vinegar, and even a pinch of freshly ground black pepper.

SOS-FREE TIP: This gazpacho recipe is great even if you pass on the oil. Feel free to omit it, but you may want to add another whole-food fat, like some diced avocado, just before serving or blend in 1 tablespoon of almond butter to aid the absorption of fat-soluble vitamins.

PER SERVING (1½ CUPS): Calories: 229; Fat: 5g; Sodium: 300mg; Carbohydrates: 40g; Fiber: 12g; Sugar: 14g; Protein: 11g

CHILLED AVOCADO, ASPARAGUS, AND CUCUMBER SOUP

SERVES 2 | **PREP TIME** 15 minutes | **COOK TIME** 5 minutes

This chilled soup will thrill your taste buds. Not only is it refreshing. Not only does it bring to mind springlike tromps through fields of flowers. It also contains so many nutrients that you really can't afford not to make it. Bonus: It's even better after a day or two in the fridge.

6 cups water, plus more as needed

8 ounces asparagus, ends trimmed, cut into 2-inch pieces

1 celery stalk, diced

Juice of 1 lemon

Grated zest of 1 lemon

1 medium garlic clove, minced

2 teaspoons white miso

1 medium cucumber, peeled and diced

1 avocado, halved, peeled, pitted, and diced

1 cup packed fresh spinach leaves

½ cup coarsely chopped fresh cilantro leaves and stems

Freshly ground black pepper

1 teaspoon extra virgin olive oil (optional)

1. Fill a large bowl with ice and cold water and set aside.

2. In a medium saucepan, bring the water to a rolling boil. Add the asparagus to the pot and cook for 3 to 5 minutes, until just tender. Drain then submerge the asparagus in the ice bath for 1 minute to stop the cooking. Place the asparagus on a dry kitchen towel or paper towels to remove any excess water.

3. In a blender, combine the asparagus, celery, lemon juice, lemon zest, garlic, miso, cucumber, avocado, spinach, and cilantro and blend until smooth. Add water, if necessary, to reach your desired consistency. Season with pepper to taste.

4. Garnish the soup by drizzling the oil on top (if using) and serve.

VARIATION TIP: To change the texture and flavor a bit, stir in some frozen, thawed corn and some fresh herbs and diced scallions after blending.

PER SERVING (1½ CUPS): Calories: 172; Fat: 11g; Sodium: 220mg; Carbohydrates: 18g; Fiber: 10g; Sugar: 6g; Protein: 6g

SPICY CHILLED CORN SOUP

SERVES 2 | **PREP TIME** 20 minutes, plus 1 hour to chill

I first created this recipe years ago as a way to use up a jumbo bag of frozen corn—and I've never looked back. It's zesty and oh so refreshing on a hot summer day. Keep a jar of this in the fridge all summer long for an afternoon pick-me-up that won't leave you feeling weighed down. Or pair it with my Roasted Summer Vegetable Sandwiches (page 65).

½ teaspoon olive oil (optional)

1 (12-ounce) bag frozen corn, thawed, divided (see Cooking tip)

2 teaspoons white miso

1 teaspoon onion powder

1 jalapeño pepper, seeded and finely diced, divided

1 garlic clove, peeled

Juice of 1 lime

Grated zest of 1 lime

½ cup water, plus more as needed

¼ cup finely chopped fresh cilantro leaves and stems

2 scallions, white and green parts, finely chopped

Sea salt

Freshly ground black pepper

1. In a blender, combine the oil (if using), half the corn, miso, onion powder, half the jalapeño, garlic, lime juice, lime zest, and water and blend until smooth. Adjust the consistency with more water, if needed.

2. Transfer the soup to a serving bowl and stir in the cilantro, scallions, the remaining jalapeño (depending on how spicy your pepper is, do a taste test), and the remaining corn. Season the soup with salt and pepper to taste.

3. Refrigerate for about 1 hour before serving, or in an airtight container for up to 5 days.

COOKING TIP: If you want to get this soup on the table faster, do not thaw the corn—use it frozen so the soup can be served immediately.

VARIATION TIP: Stir in some drained and rinsed black beans, chopped fresh tomato, and diced avocado for even more exciting flavors and textures.

PER SERVING (1½ CUPS): Calories: 179; Fat: 1g; Sodium: 190mg; Carbohydrates: 42g; Fiber: 6g; Sugar: 7g; Protein: 7g

GINGER, PEANUT, AND CARROT BISQUE

SERVES 2 | **PREP TIME** 10 minutes | **COOK TIME** 25 minutes

The Thai-inspired flavors of this creamy soup will seriously have you wanting to book a trip to Bangkok for the real thing. This recipe calls for black sesame seeds because of their authentic flavor. If you prefer to use regular sesame seeds, toast them first in a hot skillet for 3 minutes, stirring constantly, until fragrant. Make this a one-pot meal by using an immersion blender and finishing the soup right in the cooking pot.

½ medium yellow or white onion, diced

2 garlic cloves, minced

1 pound carrots, cut into ½-inch pieces

1 celery stalk, diced

2 teaspoons red miso

2½ cups Quick Umami Broth (page 110), or store-bought low-sodium vegetable broth

2 tablespoons peanut butter

2 teaspoons finely minced peeled fresh ginger

2 scallions, white and green parts, finely chopped

1 tablespoon black sesame seeds

1. Heat a medium nonstick saucepan over low heat for 5 minutes.

2. In the hot pan, combine the onion and garlic and cook for 1 to 2 minutes, stirring frequently, until they are fragrant and softened.

3. Stir in the carrots, celery, miso, broth, and peanut butter until combined thoroughly and bring the soup to a boil over medium-high heat. Reduce the heat to medium-low and gently simmer for about 15 minutes, or until the carrots are tender.

4. Remove the saucepan from the heat and add the ginger. Blend the soup using an immersion blender, mash the soup with a potato masher for a rustic texture, or carefully transfer the soup to a blender and blend until smooth.

5. Garnish the soup with the scallions and sesame seeds before serving.

VARIATION TIP: If you're like me and love exciting and spicy food, throw in a finely diced Thai red chile when you add the onion and garlic.

PER SERVING (2 CUPS): Calories: 279; Fat: 12g; Sodium: 632mg; Carbohydrates: 39g; Fiber: 10g; Sugar: 16g; Protein: 9g

CURRIED CHICKPEA, SPINACH, AND BARLEY SOUP

SERVES 2 | **PREP TIME** 10 minutes | **COOK TIME** 40 minutes

Aquafaba (Latin for "water" and "bean") is the liquid in which the chickpeas are packed in the can. It is an excellent egg white substitute used widely in vegan cooking, and it is one of the ingredients in this hearty, satisfying soup. Packed with flavor and exciting textures, it's the perfect one-pot meal for a cozy winter evening.

1 teaspoon olive oil (optional)

2 teaspoons white miso

1/2 medium yellow or white onion, diced

1 cup finely diced carrots

1 teaspoon curry powder

1 1/4 cups Quick Umami Broth (page 110), or store-bought low-sodium vegetable broth

1/2 cup pearled barley

1 (15-ounce) can no-salt-added chickpeas, undrained

2 cups packed fresh spinach leaves

2 tablespoons chopped fresh parsley leaves

1. Heat a medium nonstick saucepan over low heat for 5 minutes.

2. Pour in the oil (if using) and add the miso, onion, carrots, and curry powder. Cook for 2 to 3 minutes, stirring frequently, until the onion has softened and the curry powder and garlic are fragrant.

3. Stir in the broth and bring the soup to a boil over medium-high heat.

4. Stir in the barley, turn the heat to medium-low, and simmer for about 20 minutes, or until the barley is tender.

5. Add the chickpeas and their aquafaba and the spinach to the pot. Turn the heat to medium and cook the soup for about 5 minutes, stirring occasionally, until the spinach wilts. Stir in the parsley and serve warm.

SOS-FREE TIP: Skip the olive oil and add a few splashes of broth in its place to prevent the aromatics and spices from sticking and burning.

PER SERVING (2 CUPS): Calories: 459; Fat: 5g; Sodium: 380mg; Carbohydrates: 89g; Fiber: 23g; Sugar: 10g; Protein: 19g

CREAMY POTATO, LEEK, AND KALE SOUP

SERVES 2 | **PREP TIME** 15 minutes | **COOK TIME** 40 minutes

Whoever said comfort food needs to be unhealthy hasn't tried this recipe. It's creamy, satisfying, and chock-full of heart- and gut-healthy fiber. Curl up with a blanket and a hot bowl of this one-pot wonder on a chilly autumn evening and prepare to feel nourished.

1 teaspoon olive oil (optional)

2 teaspoons white miso

1 leek, washed thoroughly and thinly sliced

2 garlic cloves, minced

1 celery stalk, finely diced

2 russet potatoes, cut into ½-inch cubes

3 cups Quick Umami Broth (page 110), or store-bought low-sodium vegetable broth

½ teaspoon Italian seasoning

2 tablespoons almond butter

2 cups packed chopped stemmed kale

¼ cup finely chopped fresh parsley

1. Heat a medium nonstick saucepan over low heat for 5 minutes.

2. Pour in the oil (if using) and add the miso, leek, garlic, and celery. Cook for 3 to 4 minutes, stirring frequently, until the vegetables have softened.

3. Stir in the potatoes, broth, Italian seasoning, and almond butter and bring the soup to a boil over medium-high heat. Turn the heat to medium-low and simmer the soup for 15 minutes, or until the potatoes are tender. Remove the saucepan from the heat and mash the soup with a potato masher for a rustic texture.

4. Stir in the kale, return the saucepan to medium-high heat, and cook for 7 to 9 minutes, stirring occasionally, until the kale is tender and wilted.

5. Remove the saucepan from the heat, stir in the fresh parsley, and serve.

VARIATION TIP: Turn this soup into a heartier, protein-packed meal simply by adding 1 (15-ounce) can of no-salt-added white beans or chickpeas, drained and rinsed.

PER SERVING (2 CUPS): Calories: 262; Fat: 2g; Sodium: 488mg; Carbohydrates: 57g; Fiber: 8g; Sugar: 7g; Protein: 9g

SMOKY PUMPKIN AND BLACK-EYED PEA CHILI

SERVES 2 | **PREP TIME** 10 minutes | **COOK TIME** 20 minutes

Versions of chili abound. From the original in San Antonio to dozens of vegetarian versions, everyone seems to have their own special chili recipe. Here is mine and it can be yours, too. This recipe uses canned smoked jalapeño peppers, also known as chipotle chiles, as well as pantry-friendly ingredients, to create a meal in fewer than 30 minutes.

1 teaspoon olive oil (optional)

2 teaspoons white miso

½ medium yellow or white onion, diced

3 garlic cloves, minced

1 celery stalk, finely diced

1 tablespoon canned chipotle chiles in adobo sauce, minced

½ teaspoon Italian seasoning

2 cups Quick Umami Broth (page 110), or store-bought low-sodium vegetable broth

1½ cups canned pumpkin

1 (15-ounce) can no-salt-added black-eyed peas, drained and rinsed

Sea salt

Freshly ground black pepper

1. Heat a medium nonstick saucepan over low heat for 5 minutes.

2. Pour in the oil (if using) and add the miso, onion, garlic, and celery. Cook for 3 to 5 minutes, stirring frequently, until the vegetables have softened.

3. Stir in the chipotles, Italian seasoning, broth, and pumpkin and bring the soup to a boil over medium-high heat. Stir in the black-eyed peas and cook for 5 minutes, stirring occasionally.

4. Season with salt and pepper to taste and serve.

SOS-FREE TIP: This chili recipe is great even if you skip the oil and sauté your vegetables with a few tablespoons of vegetable broth instead. If you choose to skip the oil, you may want to add another whole-food fat like diced avocado just before serving or blend in 1 tablespoon of almond butter to aid the absorption of fat-soluble vitamins.

VARIATION TIP: Top this chili with diced white onion, chopped fresh cilantro, and a dollop of plant-based yogurt.

PER SERVING (2 CUPS): Calories: 280; Fat: 3g; Sodium: 492mg; Carbohydrates: 55g; Fiber: 16g; Sugar: 12g; Protein: 16g

MUSHROOM, LENTIL, AND SPINACH STEW

SERVES 2 | **PREP TIME** 10 minutes | **COOK TIME** 55 minutes

Lentils are my weeknight go-to dried legume because they don't need to be soaked overnight and can cook in fewer than 30 minutes. This protein- and fiber-filled—and, did I mention, delectable—recipe is a great way to ensure you're also eating your leafy greens.

1 teaspoon olive oil (optional)

2 teaspoons white miso

½ medium yellow or white onion, diced

2 garlic cloves, minced

1 celery stalk, finely diced

3 cups sliced white or cremini mushrooms

3 cups Quick Umami Broth (page 110), or store-bought low-sodium vegetable broth

½ teaspoon Italian seasoning

⅔ cup dried green, black, or French lentils, sorted and rinsed (see Cooking tip)

4 cups packed chopped fresh spinach

¼ cup finely chopped fresh parsley

Sea salt (optional)

Freshly ground black pepper (optional)

1. Heat a medium nonstick saucepan over low heat for 5 minutes.

2. Pour in the oil (if using) and add the miso, onion, garlic, and celery. Cook for about 5 minutes, stirring frequently, until the vegetables have softened.

3. Turn the heat to medium, add the mushrooms, and stir to combine. Cook for about 15 minutes, until the mushrooms have released their water and the liquid has reduced in volume to less than ¼ cup.

4. Stir in the broth, Italian seasoning, and lentils and bring the stew to a boil over medium-high heat. Reduce the heat to medium-low and simmer for 20 minutes, or until the lentils are tender.

5. Stir in the spinach and cook for 5 minutes, or until wilted. Remove the saucepan from the heat, stir in the parsley, season with salt (if using) and pepper (if using) to taste, and serve.

COOKING TIP: Lentils are an unprocessed agricultural product, so there may be small stones and debris in the mix. Before using them in a recipe, take a look and sort out anything that's not a lentil.

PER SERVING (2 CUPS): Calories: 314; Fat: 2g; Sodium: 511mg; Carbohydrates: 56g; Fiber: 17g; Sugar: 7g; Protein: 25g

WEEKNIGHT MOROCCAN-STYLE CHICKPEA AND LENTIL SOUP

SERVES 2 | **PREP TIME** 10 minutes | **COOK TIME** 45 minutes

This dish is inspired by one of my favorite soups: harira, a tomato-based Moroccan soup with warm spices and, often, beef or lamb. Most harira recipes also call for a lot of oil and 20, or even 30, different ingredients, which, let's face it, is a little too much to juggle for a weeknight meal. I've significantly reduced the amount of oil, removed the meat, and otherwise pared down this recipe to its most flavorful and essential ingredients to give you a delicious, healthy, and satisfying meal for two in under an hour.

1 tablespoon olive oil

½ yellow or white onion, diced

2 garlic cloves, minced

½ teaspoon sweet paprika

½ teaspoon ground cumin

½ teaspoon ground cinnamon

3½ cups Quick Umami Broth (page 110), or store-bought low-sodium vegetable broth

½ cup dried green, black, or French lentils, sorted and rinsed

1 cup canned no-salt-added diced tomatoes

¼ cup whole-grain orzo

1 cup canned no-salt-added chickpeas, drained and rinsed

Sea salt

Freshly ground black pepper

1. Heat a medium nonstick saucepan over low heat for 5 minutes.

2. Pour in the oil and add the onion, garlic, paprika, cumin, and cinnamon. Cook for 3 to 5 minutes, stirring frequently, until the vegetables have softened and the spices are fragrant.

3. Stir in the broth, lentils, and tomatoes and bring the soup to a boil over medium-high heat. Reduce the heat to medium-low and simmer for 20 minutes, or until the lentils are tender.

4. Stir in the orzo and cook for 5 minutes. Add the chickpeas to the saucepan and cook for 2 to 3 minutes. Season with salt and pepper to taste.

VARIATION TIP: Add a generous pinch of cayenne pepper with the spices, and garnish with some lemon wedges and chopped fresh parsley. Make this recipe gluten-free by substituting chickpea pasta shells for the orzo.

PER SERVING (2 CUPS): Calories: 539; Fat: 11g; Sodium: 327mg; Carbohydrates: 88g; Fiber: 24g; Sugar: 9g; Protein: 26g

ONE-POT RATATOUILLE

SERVES 2 | **PREP TIME** 10 minutes | **COOK TIME** 25 minutes

Ratatouille, unlike its namesake film, originated in Nice, France, in the 1700s. This rustic stewed veggie dish is equally delicious served hot or cold with pasta, rice, or bread. And it's a light way to use summer vegetables at the peak of their flavor. Add lentils, chickpeas, or your legume of choice to transform this into a nourishing, protein-filled, satisfying meal. It's so good, you'll want to double the recipe and freeze the leftovers for up to a month.

1 tablespoon olive oil

1 medium yellow onion, diced

3 or 4 garlic cloves, chopped

2 teaspoons white miso

3 cups coarsely chopped tomato

1 red or yellow bell pepper, coarsely chopped

2 cups cubed (½ inch) eggplant

1 medium zucchini, cut into ½-inch slices

1 tablespoon fresh thyme leaves

2 tablespoons chopped fresh basil leaves

Sea salt

Freshly ground black pepper

1. Heat a medium nonstick saucepan over low heat for 5 minutes.

2. Pour in the oil and add the onion, garlic, and miso. Cook for 2 to 3 minutes, stirring frequently, until the onion has softened and the garlic is fragrant.

3. Stir in the tomato and bell pepper and bring the ratatouille to a simmer over medium heat. Cook for 5 minutes, until the tomato breaks down and releases its water. Reduce the heat to medium-low and add the eggplant, zucchini, and thyme. Simmer for about 10 minutes, until the vegetables are cooked through.

4. Remove the saucepan from the heat, stir in the basil, and season with salt and pepper to taste.

SOS-FREE TIP: Omit the oil and sauté the vegetables with a couple tablespoons of vegetable broth and swap in another whole-food fat, like a small handful of hemp seeds. Skip the salt.

PER SERVING (1½ CUPS): Calories: 201; Fat: 8g; Sodium: 209mg; Carbohydrates: 31g; Fiber: 10g; Sugar: 18g; Protein: 7g

VEGETABLE STEW WITH DUMPLINGS

SERVES 2 | **PREP TIME** 10 minutes | **COOK TIME** 50 minutes

This cozy recipe for two is inexpensive, easily customized to what you have in the fridge or freezer, uses easy-to-find vegetables, and will not leave you hungry. Make this gluten-free by substituting a gluten-free baking flour mix for the whole-wheat flour.

2 teaspoons olive oil, divided

3 teaspoons white miso, divided

1/2 yellow or white onion, diced

1 celery stalk, finely diced

2 large carrots, cut into 1/2-inch pieces

2 russet potatoes, cut into 1/2-inch cubes

1 teaspoon Italian seasoning, divided

3 cups Quick Umami Broth (page 110), or store-bought low-sodium vegetable broth

1/2 cup whole-wheat flour

1/2 teaspoon baking powder

1/4 cup soy milk

1. Heat a medium nonstick saucepan over low heat for 5 minutes.

2. Pour in 1 teaspoon of oil and add 2 teaspoons of miso, the onion, and celery. Cook for about 5 minutes, stirring frequently, until the vegetables have softened and the onion is translucent.

3. Stir in the carrots, potatoes, 1/2 teaspoon of Italian seasoning, and the broth. Bring the stew to a boil over medium-high heat. Reduce the heat to medium-low and simmer for 15 to 20 minutes, or until the vegetables are tender.

4. While the vegetables simmer, in a small mixing bowl, stir together the flour, remaining 1 teaspoon of oil, remaining 1 teaspoon of miso, remaining 1/2 teaspoon of Italian seasoning, the baking powder, and milk to form a thick, fluffy dumpling batter. Divide the mix into four equal portions and gently drop them on top of the simmering soup. Do NOT stir the dumpling mix into the soup.

5. Cover the saucepan with a tight-fitting lid and simmer the dumplings in the broth for 10 to 15 minutes, or until a wooden toothpick inserted into the middle of a dumpling comes out clean.

PER SERVING (2 CUPS): Calories: 413; Fat: 7g; Sodium: 737mg; Carbohydrates: 81g; Fiber: 12g; Sugar: 10g; Protein: 14g

CURRIED RED SPLIT LENTIL AND POTATO STEW

SERVES 2 | **PREP TIME** 10 minutes | **COOK TIME** 30 minutes

Split or red lentils are different from other lentils because they require far less cooking time. If you need to get a hearty, flavorful, and exciting dish on the table in a flash, this Thai-inspired curry stew is a great bet and is so much healthier—and less expensive—than ordering takeout. Serve with the Fire Cider Citrus Salad (page 58) for an excellent meal.

½ teaspoon olive oil (optional)

½ yellow or white onion, diced

1 cup grated carrots

1 celery stalk, finely diced

1 tablespoon Thai red curry paste

2 Medjool dates, pitted and finely chopped

2 cups Quick Umami Broth (page 110), or store-bought low-sodium vegetable broth

1 cup canned reduced-fat coconut milk

2 cups cubed (½ inch) Yukon Gold potatoes

½ cup dried red split lentils, sorted (See Mushroom, Lentil, and Spinach Stew, Cooking tip, page 51)

2 teaspoons freshly squeezed lime juice

Sea salt (optional)

1. Heat a medium nonstick saucepan over low heat for 5 minutes.

2. Pour in the oil (if using) and add the onion, carrot, celery, and curry paste. Cook for about 5 minutes, stirring frequently, until the vegetables have softened and the curry paste is fragrant.

3. Stir in the dates, broth, coconut milk, potatoes, and lentils and bring the stew to a boil over medium-high heat. Reduce the heat to medium-low and simmer the stew for 15 minutes, until the potatoes are tender.

4. Remove the saucepan from the heat, stir in the lime juice, season with salt (if using) to taste, and serve.

VARIATION TIP: Take this dish to the next level by garnishing with some chopped fresh cilantro or adding some extra heat with fresh Thai red chiles.

PER SERVING (2 CUPS): Calories: 498; Fat: 8g; Sodium: 635mg; Carbohydrates: 96g; Fiber: 11g; Sugar: 25g; Protein: 18g

Fire Cider Citrus Salad 58

Chapter Five

SALADS AND SANDWICHES

FIRE CIDER CITRUS SALAD

SERVES 2 | **PREP TIME** 25 minutes

Fire cider has been an indispensable folk remedy for the common cold and an overall elixir for when you're feeling a little under the weather. This recipe takes the ingredients commonly found in fire cider and transforms them into an exciting flavor bomb of a salad. If you're a fan of big, bold, adventurous flavors, you're going to LOVE this recipe. I eat this salad topped with hulled hemp seeds or chopped walnuts for additional heart-healthy fats, minerals, and fiber.

2 tablespoons apple cider vinegar

1 teaspoon peeled and grated fresh ginger

1 garlic clove, finely minced

1/2 teaspoon peeled and grated fresh horseradish root

2 scallions, white and green parts, finely chopped

2 teaspoons finely minced jalapeño pepper

1 avocado, peeled, halved, pitted, and cubed

6 cups finely chopped stemmed curly kale leaves

2 navel oranges, peeled and segmented

1/2 cup finely chopped cilantro leaves and stems

Sea salt (optional)

Freshly ground black pepper

1. In a large salad bowl, combine the vinegar, ginger, garlic, horseradish, scallions, jalapeño, and avocado and mash to form a smooth paste.

2. Add the kale to the bowl and massage the kale with your hands for about 3 minutes to soften the kale and thoroughly incorporate the dressing.

3. Add the orange segments and cilantro and season with salt (if using) and pepper to taste. Gently stir them into the salad and serve.

COOKING TIP: Have you ever been served a bowl of raw kale and spent an eternity trying to chew it? Massaging fibrous leafy greens, like curly kale, can make them a lot easier to eat in a raw dish like this. Be sure to chop the kale finely and don't be afraid to roll up your sleeves, get your hands in the bowl, and squeeze it firmly as you're massaging. If you prefer not to massage the kale, choose lacinato (dinosaur) kale for its more tender texture.

VARIATION TIP: Instead of using salt, add 1 teaspoon of white miso with the aromatics.

PER SERVING (1 1/2 CUPS): Calories: 220; Fat: 12g; Sodium: 51mg; Carbohydrates: 29g; Fiber: 11g; Sugar: 14g; Protein: 5g

SPICED PEAR AND SPINACH SALAD

SERVES 2 | **PREP TIME** 20 minutes

Pears (Bosc works great here) are the perfect sweet to this savory salad; chock-full of vitamins and minerals, pears are one of the highest fiber fruits around. If you're having trouble finding ripe fruit, swap the pears for equally delicious crisp, sweet apples like Fuji, Gala, or Honeycrisp.

3 tablespoons apple cider vinegar, plus more as needed

1 teaspoon peeled and grated fresh ginger

1 garlic clove, finely minced

2 scallions, white and green parts, finely chopped

2 tablespoons almond butter

¼ teaspoon ground cinnamon

2 tablespoons water, divided

4 cups lightly packed finely chopped stemmed fresh spinach leaves

2 large ripe pears, cored and coarsely chopped

Sea salt (optional)

Freshly ground black pepper (optional)

1. In a large salad bowl, whisk the vinegar, ginger, garlic, scallions, almond butter, and cinnamon to create the dressing. Thin the dressing with 1 tablespoon of water and let sit for 5 minutes. Readjust the consistency with the remaining 1 tablespoon of water or more vinegar, depending on your taste.

2. Add the spinach and pears to the bowl, gently toss to coat, season with salt (if using) and pepper (if using) to taste, and serve.

COOKING TIP: Reduce prep time by purchasing prewashed baby spinach greens.

PER SERVING (2 CUPS): Calories: 256; Fat: 9g; Sodium: 60mg; Carbohydrates: 43g; Fiber: 11g; Sugar: 24g; Protein: 6g

GRAPE, WALNUT, AND ARUGULA HARVEST SALAD

SERVES 2 | **PREP TIME** 20 minutes

Walnuts are a much-vaunted superfood. They are so nutritious, in fact, that scientists gather every year in California for a walnut conference to confer about the latest nutritional findings. For this reason, use them whenever you can; here's one opportunity. This recipe has a little of everything: sweet juicy grapes, peppery arugula, tart balsamic vinegar, and rich, creamy walnut butter. Serve with my Ginger, Peanut, and Carrot Bisque (page 47) for a mouthwatering meal.

2 tablespoons balsamic vinegar

1 small garlic clove, finely minced

2 teaspoons Dijon mustard

2 tablespoons walnut butter

2 teaspoons white miso

1½ cups halved red seedless grapes

¼ medium red onion, thinly sliced

3 cups chopped fresh arugula leaves

Freshly ground black pepper

3 tablespoons chopped walnuts

In a large salad bowl, whisk the vinegar, garlic, mustard, walnut butter, and miso to blend. Add the grapes and onion and stir to coat thoroughly. Add the arugula and gently fold it into the salad. Season with pepper to taste, top with the walnuts, and serve immediately.

VARIATION TIP: To turn this salad into a complete meal, add some no-salt-added drained and rinsed black beans or chickpeas for a serious fiber- and protein-packed entrée.

PER SERVING (2 CUPS): Calories: 294; Fat: 18g; Sodium: 315mg; Carbohydrates: 32g; Fiber: 5g; Sugar: 23g; Protein: 7g

CURRIED BRUSSELS SPROUT SLAW

SERVES 2 | **PREP TIME** 25 minutes

These cruciferous mini-cabbagelike veggies boast four times the amount of vitamin C as an orange in a single serving. As if that isn't reason enough to indulge, this recipe uses creamy avocado alongside zesty aromatics and curry spices to create a flavorful lunch in just minutes. This recipe puts that old-fashioned notion to rest that slaw needs to be swimming in mayonnaise for it to be delicious.

2 tablespoons apple cider vinegar

1 teaspoon peeled and grated fresh ginger

1 garlic clove, finely minced

¼ teaspoon curry powder

1 avocado, peeled, halved, pitted, and cubed

4 cups finely shredded Brussels sprouts

2 scallions, white and green parts, finely chopped

2 medium carrots, grated

½ cup finely chopped fresh cilantro leaves and stems

Sea salt

Freshly ground black pepper

1. In a large salad bowl, combine the vinegar, ginger, garlic, curry powder, and avocado. Mash to form a smooth paste.

2. Add the Brussels sprouts, scallions, carrots, and cilantro and gently stir them into the dressing. Season with salt and pepper to taste and serve.

VARIATION TIP: Raisins are a polarizing ingredient— you either love 'em or hate 'em. But in this dish, they do add just the right touch of sweetness, so, if you love 'em, I highly recommend adding a handful.

PER SERVING (2 CUPS): Calories: 313; Fat: 19g; Sodium: 738mg; Carbohydrates: 34g; Fiber: 13g; Sugar: 8g; Protein: 8g

MARINATED LENTIL, HERB, AND KALE SALAD

SERVES 2 | **PREP TIME** 20 minutes | **COOK TIME** 25 minutes

Get ready to fall in love with one of my favorite hearty, nutrient-dense legumes—the mighty lentil. Loaded with fiber, folic acid, potassium, and protein, lentils are one of your best bets for packing a lot of nutrition into your meal plans. And although, technically, you could use canned lentils to make this dish in fewer than 30 minutes, you really can't beat the price, shelf life, and ease of cooking dried lentils yourself.

2 cups water

½ cup dried green, black, or French lentils, rinsed and sorted (See Mushroom, Lentil, and Spinach Stew, Cooking tip, page 51)

¼ cup red wine vinegar

1 garlic clove, finely minced

1 teaspoon white miso

2 tablespoons tahini

2 tablespoons chopped fresh thyme leaves

2 scallions, white and green parts, finely chopped

6 cups finely chopped stemmed curly kale leaves (see Fire Cider Citrus Salad, Cooking tip, page 58) ▷

1. In a medium nonstick saucepan, bring the water to a rolling boil. Stir in the lentils, return the water to a boil, then reduce the heat to medium-low and gently simmer for 15 to 20 minutes, until the lentils are tender but not mushy.

2. While the lentils cook, in a large salad bowl, whisk the vinegar, garlic, miso, tahini, thyme, and scallions to blend.

3. Add the kale to the salad bowl and massage it with your hands for about 3 minutes to soften the kale and thoroughly incorporate the dressing. Set aside.

4. Drain the cooked lentils thoroughly and let cool for about 10 minutes. Once slightly cooled, add the lentils to the salad bowl and toss to coat thoroughly.

**½ cup finely chopped
fresh parsley leaves
and stems**

**¼ cup chopped fresh
oregano leaves**

Sea salt (optional)

**Freshly ground black
pepper (optional)**

5. Place the kale and lentil mixture in an airtight container and refrigerate until just ready to serve, or up to 2 days in advance.

6. When ready to serve, gently fold in the parsley and oregano and season with salt (if using) and pepper (if using) to taste.

COOKING TIP: This dish is delightful served immediately while still a little warm, but also when allowed to marinate in the refrigerator for a few hours or overnight so the lentils absorb the marinade and the flavors intensify. And although fresh herbs are better for this recipe, in a pinch, you can substitute ½ teaspoon of dried parsley, ¼ teaspoon of dried thyme, and ¼ teaspoon of dried oregano.

PER SERVING (2 CUPS): Calories: 315; Fat: 10g; Sodium: 155mg; Carbohydrates: 42g; Fiber: 16g; Sugar: 2g; Protein: 19g

GOLDEN BEET, APPLE, AND BARLEY SLAW

SERVES 2 | **PREP TIME** 15 minutes | **COOK TIME** 35 minutes

Beets can be an earthy, sweet addition to a salad, but they can also taste like a handful of dirt, am I right? This dish serves up big, bold flavors and exciting textures, and it balances the beets' earthiness with fresh, bright notes of lemon and ginger to win over even the harshest beet critic.

2 cups water

½ cup dried pearled barley, rinsed

3 tablespoons freshly squeezed lemon juice

1 teaspoon peeled and grated fresh ginger

1 teaspoon white miso

1½ tablespoons sunflower seed butter

2 scallions, white and green parts, finely chopped

2 medium sweet, crisp apples (Fuji, Gala, Honeycrisp), cored and grated

2 medium golden beets, peeled and grated

¼ cup sultanas (also known as golden raisins)

½ cup finely chopped fresh cilantro leaves and stems

Freshly ground black pepper

1. In a medium nonstick saucepan, bring the water to a rolling boil. Stir in the barley, return the water to a boil, then reduce the heat to medium-low and gently simmer for 25 to 30 minutes, or until the barley is tender. Drain the water from the barley and let the grains cool slightly for 10 minutes.

2. While the barley cooks, in a large salad bowl, whisk the lemon juice, ginger, miso, and sunflower seed butter to form a smooth paste.

3. Add the scallions, apples, beets, sultanas, cilantro, and cooked barley and gently toss to coat thoroughly. Season with pepper to taste before serving.

COOKING TIP: I use pearled barley for this recipe because of how quickly it cooks. If you're looking for a more whole and intact grain, swap the pearled barley for whole barley or even other hearty and toothsome grains like farro and increase the time it simmers to about 45 minutes.

VARIATION TIP: Add some finely minced jalapeño pepper for an exciting and spicy kick. Or use cooked/roasted beets rather than raw, and add them in step 2.

PER SERVING (1½ CUPS): Calories: 452; Fat: 8g; Sodium: 175mg; Carbohydrates: 93g; Fiber: 17g; Sugar: 40g; Protein: 10g

ROASTED SUMMER VEGETABLE SANDWICHES

SERVES 2 | **PREP TIME** 10 minutes | **COOK TIME** 20 minutes

These sandwiches feature meaty mushrooms—which are equally impressive when roasted in the oven or cooked on an outdoor grill—and a creamy hummus-style spread that will have you craving them year-round.

1 tablespoon neutral cooking oil (like vegetable or sunflower seed oil)

1½ cups Tomato and Herb Dressing (page 116), or store-bought low-sodium Italian dressing, divided

2 large portobello mushroom caps, washed and dried

1 medium eggplant, cut into ½-inch planks

1 red bell pepper, halved and seeded

½ medium white or yellow onion, cut into ½-inch slices

1 cup no-salt-added chickpeas, drained and rinsed

4 slices whole-grain bread

1 cup lightly packed fresh baby spinach leaves

Freshly ground black pepper

1. Preheat the oven to 400°F. Line a baking sheet with parchment paper or a silicone baking mat.

2. In a large mixing bowl, combine the oil and ½ cup of dressing to create the marinade. Add the mushrooms, eggplant, bell pepper, and onion to the bowl and gently toss the vegetables to coat. Arrange the vegetables on the prepared baking sheet, evenly spaced.

3. Roast for about 20 minutes, or until the vegetables are soft, tender, and browned.

4. While the vegetables roast, in a small mixing bowl, combine ½ cup of dressing with the chickpeas and smash with the back of a fork to create a rustic, hummuslike consistency.

5. In the same large bowl used for the vegetables, combine the remaining ½ cup of dressing and the roasted vegetables. Toss the vegetables to coat.

6. To assemble the sandwich, toast the bread lightly.

7. Spread the mashed chickpeas on one side of each piece of bread. Layer the roasted vegetables and the baby spinach over the chickpeas, season with pepper to taste, and top the sandwiches with the remaining bread slices to serve.

PER SERVING (1 SANDWICH): Calories: 659; Fat: 23g; Sodium: 512mg; Carbohydrates: 93g; Fiber: 27g; Sugar: 28g; Protein: 28g

SMOKY LENTIL SLOPPY JOES

SERVES 2 | **PREP TIME** 15 minutes | **COOK TIME** 40 minutes

Umami is a Japanese word that means "essence of deliciousness" and is used to describe savory and meaty dishes. This traditionally meat-centric and picky eater–friendly meal features plenty of savory ingredients in a protein-packed and satisfying sandwich without the cholesterol and saturated fats found in meat-based sloppy Joes. Eat it and you, too, will experience the essence of deliciousness.

1 tablespoon neutral cooking oil (like vegetable or sunflower seed oil)

1 garlic clove, finely minced

1 medium white or yellow onion, finely diced

1/8 teaspoon cayenne pepper (optional)

1/2 teaspoon smoked paprika

1 teaspoon red miso

1 cup finely diced shiitake mushroom caps

2 tablespoons tomato paste

1 1/2 cups Quick Umami Broth (page 110), or store-bought low-sodium vegetable broth

1/2 cup dried green, black, or French lentils, rinsed and sorted (See Mushroom, Lentil, and Spinach Stew, Cooking tip, page 51) ▶

1. Preheat a medium nonstick saucepan over medium-low heat for 5 minutes.

2. Pour in the oil and add the garlic, onion, cayenne (if using), smoked paprika, and miso. Cook for 3 to 5 minutes, until the spices are fragrant and the onion is translucent and slightly browned.

3. Add the mushrooms and cook for 5 minutes, until the mushrooms release their moisture and it has evaporated. Stir in the tomato paste and cook for 2 to 3 minutes.

4. Add the broth and bring the soup to a rolling boil over medium-high heat.

5. Stir in the lentils and cook for about 20 minutes, or until most of the broth has been absorbed and the lentils have thickened slightly.

6. Remove the saucepan from the heat, stir in the vinegar, and season with salt and black pepper to taste.

2 tablespoons apple cider vinegar

Sea salt

Freshly ground black pepper

Toasted whole-wheat buns or lettuce leaves, for serving

7. Serve on toasted buns or a bed of lettuce or alone as a chili.

VARIATION TIP: Swap the green lentils for red split lentils, which cook in only 7 to 10 minutes, and cut your cooking time in half.

PER SERVING (1 CUP): Calories: 305; Fat: 8g; Sodium: 265mg; Carbohydrates: 45g; Fiber: 12g; Sugar: 6g; Protein: 16g

QUICK CHICKPEA FALAFEL BURGERS

SERVES 2 | **PREP TIME** 15 minutes | **COOK TIME** 15 minutes

Ahhh, falafel, the delectable and quintessential Middle Eastern street food, but whose origins are claimed by so many countries. Most traditional falafel recipes call for soaking dried chickpeas overnight. But if you're anything like me and forget to soak your beans, I've got you covered with this fast, easy, and flavorful falafel burger recipe. Serve these falafel burgers with the sauce in a whole-grain pita, between slices of whole-grain bread, or as a topper for a dinner salad. Get creative with the toppings, too, like shredded lettuce, a dollop of spicy harissa, and pickled red onions.

4 tablespoons Veggie Magic Sauce (page 111; see Variation tip), divided

1 tablespoon freshly squeezed lemon juice

¼ cup unsweetened plant-based yogurt (like unsweetened Greek-style almond yogurt)

1 (15-ounce) can no-salt-added chickpeas, drained, rinsed, and patted dry

½ cup finely diced red onion

2 garlic cloves, finely minced

1 teaspoon ground cumin

2 tablespoons neutral cooking oil (like vegetable or sunflower seed oil), divided ▶

1. In a small bowl, whisk 2 tablespoons of veggie magic sauce, the lemon juice, and yogurt to blend and refrigerate until ready to serve.

2. In a medium mixing bowl, combine the chickpeas, onion, garlic, cumin, 1 tablespoon of oil, the parsley, cilantro, flour, and remaining 2 tablespoons of veggie magic sauce. Mash until the mixture comes together to form a cohesive ball with a slightly rustic texture. Taste and season with salt and pepper, if needed. Divide the mixture in half and form each portion into a ¾-inch-thick falafel patty.

3. Preheat a medium nonstick skillet on low heat for 5 minutes.

1/4 cup finely chopped
fresh parsley leaves

1/4 cup finely chopped
fresh cilantro leaves
and stems

1 tablespoon
whole-wheat flour

Sea salt

Freshly ground
black pepper

4. Add the remaining 1 tablespoon of oil to the skillet
and heat until it shimmers. Add the falafel patties
to the skillet and cook for 5 minutes per side, or
until golden brown. Serve as desired.

SOS-FREE TIP: Take the oil out of the recipe and bake
the patties on a parchment paper–lined baking sheet
at 375°F for 20 to 25 minutes, until golden brown. Skip
the salt.

VARIATION TIP: If you're short on time, replace the
Veggie Magic Sauce (page 111) with 2 tablespoons of
tahini and adjust the sauce with a pinch of miso or salt
and pepper to taste.

PER SERVING (1 BURGER PATTY AND 1/4 CUP SAUCE):
Calories: 527; Fat: 30g; Sodium: 139mg; Carbohydrates: 52g; Fiber: 16g;
Sugar: 7g; Protein: 19g

BAKED ARTICHOKE "CRAB" CAKE SANDWICHES

SERVES 2 | **PREP TIME** 20 minutes | **COOK TIME** 20 minutes

Missing those crab cakes so reminiscent of summers at the beach? No need. Not only does the texture of chopped artichoke hearts resemble crabmeat, other ingredients, such as dulse flakes (a seaweed), add a taste of the ocean and are a good source of calcium, fiber, iodine, iron, magnesium, protein, and zinc. I prefer to use frozen artichokes because most of those you find in a can or a jar are swimming in salt and oil.

1 celery stalk, very finely chopped

2 scallions, white and green parts, finely chopped, divided

4 tablespoons finely chopped fresh dill, divided

1 teaspoon dulse flakes (see Variation tip)

1 cup frozen, thawed coarsely chopped artichoke hearts

1 tablespoon olive oil

4 tablespoons Veggie Magic Sauce (page 111), divided (see Variation tip)

2 tablespoons chickpea flour, plus more as needed ▶

1. Preheat the oven to 400°F. Line a baking sheet with parchment paper or a silicone baking mat.

2. In a medium mixing bowl, combine the celery, half the scallions, 2 tablespoons of dill, the dulse flakes, artichokes, oil, and 2 tablespoons of veggie magic sauce. Stir thoroughly.

3. Add the flour and stir again to combine. Add more flour, if needed, to bring the mixture together into a firm and cohesive ball with your hands. Divide the artichoke mixture into four equal portions and roll each portion into a ball. Arrange the "crab" cakes on the prepared baking sheet, spaced evenly, and gently press down to flatten and form ½-inch-thick cakes.

4. Bake for 10 minutes. Flip the cakes and bake for about 10 minutes more, or until golden brown.

5. While the cakes bake, in a medium mixing bowl, stir together the remaining scallions, remaining 2 tablespoons of dill, remaining 2 tablespoons of sauce, and the lemon juice. Season the sauce with salt and pepper to taste. Reserve half of this sauce for the sandwiches.

1 tablespoon freshly
squeezed lemon juice

Sea salt

Freshly ground
black pepper

2 cups finely shredded
purple cabbage

2 whole-grain bread
slices, pitas, or tortillas
(optional)

6. Add the cabbage to the bowl with the sauce and toss to coat thoroughly.

7. Serve these cakes alone, on whole-grain bread, in a pita, or wrapped in a tortilla with the slaw and sauce.

COOKING TIP: These cakes can be a little fragile. Be gentle when transferring them off the baking sheet and/or refrigerate them overnight, if you can, before baking to let them firm up.

VARIATION TIP: If you can't find dulse flakes, use very finely chopped nori or ½ teaspoon of store-bought vegan "fish sauce." And if you don't have time to make the Veggie Magic Sauce (page 111), just use 2 tablespoons of tahini and another tablespoon of lemon juice instead.

PER SERVING (2 CAKES, 1 CUP SLAW, 1 TABLESPOON REMAINING SAUCE): Calories: 247; Fat: 15g; Sodium: 230mg; Carbohydrates: 24g; Fiber: 9g; Sugar: 6g; Protein: 9g

WHITE BEAN–PESTO COLLARD WRAPS

SERVES 2 | **PREP TIME** 25 minutes | **COOK TIME** 5 minutes

De-glutenize your sandwich and go for this lighter lunch alternative: the delicious collard wrap. Filled with heart-healthy fats, fiber, protein, and three servings of vegetables, each wrap packs a nutrient-dense punch with tons of fresh flavors.

3 cups water

2 large collard leaves, stems trimmed

1 (15-ounce) can no-salt-added white beans, drained and rinsed

½ cup Herb Pesto (page 118), or store-bought plant-based pesto

¼ cup finely chopped red onion

2 medium carrots, grated (optional)

1 celery stalk, finely diced

Sea salt

Freshly ground black pepper

1. Fill a large bowl with ice and cold water and set aside.

2. In a large nonstick skillet, bring the water to a boil over medium-high heat. Place the collard leaves flat in the skillet and boil for about 1 minute per side, or until they are tender. Immediately transfer the cooked collards to the ice bath to preserve their bright-green color and stop the cooking. Remove the collards from the water, pat dry, and shave down the thickness of the remaining stem with a paring knife to make it flexible enough for rolling and stuffing.

3. In a medium mixing bowl, combine the beans, pesto, onion, carrots (if using), and celery and slightly mash the beans. Season with salt and pepper to taste.

4. To assemble the wraps, place one collard leaf on a work surface with the stem facing toward you. Place half of the bean mixture in the middle of the leaf and fold the bottom of the collard up and over to cover the beans. Then, fold in both sides toward the center, and roll the leaf away from you, creating the wrap. Repeat with the remaining leaf and filling. Halve each wrap and serve immediately.

PER SERVING (1 WRAP): Calories: 318; Fat: 11g; Sodium: 125mg; Carbohydrates: 40g; Fiber: 13g; Sugar: 3g; Protein: 16g

SWEET POTATO AND BLACK BEAN BURGERS

SERVES 2 | **PREP TIME** 15 minutes | **COOK TIME** 25 minutes

No collection of plant-based recipes would be complete without a versatile and delicious black bean burger recipe. Serve these burgers alone, on a bed of grains, or, if gluten isn't an issue, on toasted whole-grain bread with your choice of toppings, like quick-pickled red onions or roasted red bell peppers, and slather on flavor-packed spreads like my Herb Pesto (page 118).

1 tablespoon chia seeds

3 tablespoons water

1 (15-ounce) can no-salt-added black beans, drained and rinsed

½ cup quick-cooking oats

¼ cup finely diced red onion

2 garlic cloves, finely minced

1 medium roasted sweet potato, peeled (see Variation tip)

1 tablespoon sunflower seed butter or tahini

1 tablespoon nutritional yeast

1 teaspoon white miso

1 teaspoon salt-free all-purpose seasoning

1. Preheat the oven to 375°F. Line a baking sheet with parchment paper or a silicone baking mat.

2. In a small bowl, stir together the chia seeds and water to create the binding mixture. Set aside for at least 10 minutes to thicken.

3. In a medium mixing bowl, combine the beans, oats, onion, garlic, sweet potato, sunflower seed butter, nutritional yeast, miso, and seasoning. Using your hands, massage and combine the burger mixture until it forms a rustic paste. Add the chia seed binder and mix to combine thoroughly. Divide the burger mixture in half, shape each portion into a patty, ½ inch thick, and place on the prepared baking sheet.

4. Bake for about 15 minutes. Flip the burgers and bake for about 10 minutes more, until firm to the touch and slightly browned on both sides.

USE IT AGAIN: Double this recipe and wrap leftovers tightly and freeze them for up to 1 month.

VARIATION TIP: To make these burgers for a quick weeknight dinner, substitute ½ cup of canned pumpkin for the roasted sweet potato.

PER SERVING (1 BURGER PATTY): Calories: 433; Fat: 8g; Sodium: 148mg; Carbohydrates: 70g; Fiber: 20g; Sugar: 5g; Protein: 21g

Lemony Spring Vegetable and Farro Bowl 78

Chapter Six

MAIN MEALS

WARM ROASTED GARLIC AND TOMATO HUMMUS WITH ROASTED CAULIFLOWER

SERVES 2 | **PREP TIME** 25 minutes | **COOK TIME** 30 minutes

This dish is one of my favorites because it is scrumptious and healthy, completely worth a little bit of time investment. The hummus swaps oil for aquafaba, the starchy liquid that comes in the can of cannellini beans (and chickpeas) and one of plant-based eating's best secrets. This meal can be divided into two equal portions and plated separately or get garlicky together and serve it on a larger platter to share for a fun, intimate dinner for two.

1 (15-ounce) can no-salt-added cannellini beans, drained, aquafaba reserved

2 teaspoons white miso, divided

1 teaspoon dried Italian seasoning

1 medium head cauliflower, cut into 1½-inch florets

2 Roma tomatoes, halved

3 or 4 garlic cloves, unpeeled

2 tablespoons sunflower seed butter

3 tablespoons finely chopped fresh parsley, divided

3 tablespoons finely chopped fresh basil, divided

¼ teaspoon red pepper flakes

1. Preheat the oven to 400°F. Line a baking sheet with parchment paper or a silicone baking mat.

2. In a small mixing bowl, whisk the aquafaba, 1 teaspoon of miso, and Italian seasoning to blend.

3. In a large mixing bowl, combine the cauliflower, tomatoes, and garlic. Add ⅓ cup of the aquafaba mixture to the vegetables and gently toss to coat. Reserve the remaining aquafaba mixture. Transfer the vegetables to the prepared baking sheet, evenly spaced.

4. Roast for 30 minutes, or until the cauliflower is tender, the tomatoes have softened, and the garlic has roasted.

5. While the vegetables roast, in a medium mixing bowl, combine the drained beans, remaining 1 teaspoon of miso, the sunflower seed butter, 2 tablespoons of parsley, 2 tablespoons of basil, and red pepper flakes. Using the back of a fork, mash the ingredients to form a rustic and thick bean paste. Set the bean paste aside.

6. In a small saucepan over medium heat, heat the remaining aquafaba mixture for about 5 minutes, or until simmering. Add the bean mixture from step 5 to the saucepan and stir to combine. Reduce the heat to low and keep the hummus warm until the vegetables are roasted.

7. Remove the vegetables from the oven. Peel the roasted garlic cloves and smash them into a paste. Add the garlic paste and the roasted tomatoes to the hummus and mix to combine thoroughly. Serve immediately by spreading the hummus in an even layer on the plate or platter and top with the roasted cauliflower and remaining 1 tablespoon of parsley and remaining 1 tablespoon of basil.

COOKING TIP: Depending on the season and quality of your tomatoes, you may want to add a tablespoon or two of red wine vinegar to the hummus for an extra splash of brightness and flavor.

PER SERVING (1 CUP HUMMUS AND 2 CUPS CAULIFLOWER):
Calories: 379; Fat: 11g; Sodium: 287mg; Carbohydrates: 55g; Fiber: 20g; Sugar: 12g; Protein: 21g

LEMONY SPRING VEGETABLE AND FARRO BOWL

SERVES 2 | **PREP TIME** 10 minutes | **COOK TIME** 25 minutes

Farro, a nutty, hearty, and versatile ancient (found in the tombs of Egyptian kings) whole grain, is the star of this bright, flavorful seasonal dish. Gluten-free? Swap the farro for quinoa or brown rice.

2½ cups Quick Umami Broth (page 110), or store-bought low-sodium vegetable broth, divided

¾ cup dried pearled farro

¼ cup Veggie Magic Sauce (page 111; see Variation tip)

8 ounces asparagus, trimmed and cut into 1-inch pieces

1⅓ cups frozen green peas, thawed

4 cups chopped fresh spinach

Juice of 1 lemon

Sea salt (optional)

Freshly ground black pepper

Grated zest of 1 lemon

1. In a small nonstick saucepan, bring 2 cups of broth to a rolling boil. Stir in the farro, cover the pot, and simmer on medium-low heat for about 20 minutes, or until the farro is tender.

2. While the farro cooks, in a medium nonstick saucepan, stir together the remaining ½ cup of broth and the veggie magic sauce. Bring to a gentle simmer over medium heat. Stir in the asparagus, cover the pan, and cook for 3 minutes. Add the peas, re-cover the pan, and cook for 3 minutes more. Fold in the spinach and cook for 3 to 5 minutes to wilt, stirring frequently.

3. Remove the vegetables from the heat, stir in the lemon juice, and season with salt (if using) and pepper to taste.

4. Drain any excess liquid from the cooked farro and stir in the lemon zest. Divide the farro into two bowls and top with the cooked vegetables.

VARIATION TIP: Take this dish to the next level by adding some chopped fresh chives, dill, oregano, or parsley. If you're short on time, replace the Veggie Magic Sauce (page 111) with 2 tablespoons of tahini and 1 tablespoon of freshly squeezed lemon juice.

PER SERVING (3 CUPS): Calories: 488; Fat: 11g; Sodium: 469mg; Carbohydrates: 84g; Fiber: 20g; Sugar: 11g; Protein: 21g

MAC AND CHEESE WITH WILTED GREENS

SERVES 2 | **PREP TIME** 10 minutes | **COOK TIME** 20 minutes

Plant-based does not equal no mac and cheese. You just have to get a little creative. Grab a batch of Cheesy Sauce (page 112), some frozen green leafy vegetables, and the whole-grain or gluten-free pasta of your choice and you'll be off to comfort food heaven. Don't have elbow macaroni in the cupboard? Feel free to use penne, rotini, or even spaghetti if you're in a pasta pinch.

1½ cups dried whole-grain elbow macaroni

2 cups Cheesy Sauce (page 112)

¼ cup nutritional yeast

1 tablespoon olive oil (optional)

2 cups frozen chopped spinach or kale

Sea salt

Freshly ground black pepper

1. In a medium nonstick saucepan, cook the pasta according to the package instructions just until al dente, with a slightly chewy texture. Drain the pasta, reserving 2 cups of the pasta water.

2. Return the empty saucepan to the stovetop, pour in the cheesy sauce, and add the nutritional yeast and oil (if using). Bring to a simmer over medium heat.

3. Stir in the spinach and return the sauce to a simmer over medium-high heat, stirring frequently. Remove the saucepan from the heat, fold in the cooked pasta, and add about ½ cup of reserved pasta water to ensure that the sauce can coat the pasta thoroughly. Adjust the consistency of your final dish with the remaining pasta water, 1 to 2 tablespoons at a time, and season with salt and pepper to taste.

COOKING TIP: When adding the reserved cooking water to the pasta and sauce, keep in mind that you can always add a splash more; it's a lot harder to get rid of it once it's in there. In other words, add the water gradually.

PER SERVING (1½ CUPS): Calories: 557; Fat: 8g; Sodium: 287mg; Carbohydrates: 97g; Fiber: 21g; Sugar: 7g; Protein: 35g

ROASTED CAULIFLOWER STEAK AND MUSHROOMS

SERVES 2 | **PREP TIME** 5 minutes | **COOK TIME** 30 minutes

Break out the steak knives and enjoy this fun, steakhouse-like cauliflower and mushroom dish. Okay, so you won't be fooling anyone into thinking it's actually meat, but you will probably agree that the mushrooms make this dish a meaty, satisfying alternative to beef. I recommend serving this with Garlic Mashed Root Vegetables (page 38) for a cozy, comforting "meat-and-potatoes" dinner.

½ medium head cauliflower, cut lengthwise through the core into 2 (¾-inch) "steaks"

2 tablespoons olive oil, divided

Sea salt

Freshly ground black pepper

1 medium yellow or white onion, diced

1 tablespoon red miso

1 garlic clove, finely minced

12 ounces brown or white button mushrooms, washed and quartered

½ teaspoon dried Italian seasoning

¼ cup sherry vinegar

2 teaspoons Dijon mustard

1. Preheat the oven to 400°F. Line a baking sheet with parchment paper or a silicone baking mat.

2. Brush both sides of the cauliflower with 1 tablespoon of oil, generously season each side with salt and pepper to taste, and arrange the cauliflower "steaks" on the prepared baking sheet.

3. Roast for 15 to 20 minutes, until tender and slightly browned, flipping once after 10 minutes.

4. While the cauliflower roasts, heat a large nonstick skillet over medium-low heat for 5 minutes.

5. Pour in the remaining 1 tablespoon of oil and add the onion, miso, garlic, and a pinch of salt to the skillet. Cook for about 5 minutes, until the onion is translucent and slightly browned.

6. Add the mushrooms and Italian seasoning to the skillet and cook over medium-high heat for about 10 minutes, or until the mushrooms' liquid has released into the pan and has reduced in volume to about ½ cup. Stir in the vinegar and mustard and cook for 5 minutes, or until the vinegar has been reduced in volume by half and there is about ½ cup of sauce in the pan with the mushrooms. Season with more pepper to taste.

7. Transfer the cauliflower steaks to plates and top each with mushrooms and sauce.

COOKING TIP: Cook water-rich foods, such as mushrooms, in a wide skillet to increase the surface area and speed up the evaporation process.

PER SERVING (1 STEAK AND 1 CUP MUSHROOMS WITH SAUCE):
Calories: 240; Fat: 15g; Sodium: 535mg; Carbohydrates: 24g; Fiber: 6g; Sugar: 13g; Protein: 10g

UNSTUFFED PEPPERS

SERVES 2 | **PREP TIME** 20 minutes | **COOK TIME** 30 minutes

This "unstuffed" recipe features all the delicious flavors and exciting textures found in stuffed peppers, but in a way that uses only one saucepan. Be sure to make batches of Easy Marinara (page 114), Quick Umami Broth (page 110), and Versatile Vegetable Rice Pilaf (page 37) ahead, so you can get this on the table on a busy night even faster than pizza delivery.

1 cup Easy Marinara (page 114), or store-bought low-sodium marinara sauce

1/2 cup dried green, French, or black lentils, rinsed and sorted (See Mushroom, Lentil, and Spinach Stew, Cooking tip, page 51)

1 cup Quick Umami Broth (page 110), or store-bought low-sodium vegetable broth

1 cup frozen spinach, thawed

1 cup Versatile Vegetable Rice Pilaf (page 37)

2 large red bell peppers, cut into 1/2-inch pieces

Sea salt (optional)

Freshly ground black pepper

1. In a medium nonstick saucepan, combine the marinara, lentils, and broth and bring to a boil over medium-high heat. Reduce the heat to medium-low and simmer for about 20 minutes, or until the lentils are just tender.

2. Gently stir in the spinach and pilaf and heat thoroughly.

3. Add the bell peppers to the pan and bring the mixture to a simmer, still over medium-high heat. Season with salt (if using) and pepper and to taste, then remove from the heat. Serve hot or cold.

COOKING TIP: I add the bell peppers toward the end of cooking, so they still have a tender, slightly crisp, texture and also to preserve more of their vitamin C content, which is very heat-sensitive. You could also add them after the dish is warmed.

PER SERVING (2 CUPS): Calories: 383; Fat: 4g; Sodium: 329mg; Carbohydrates: 72g; Fiber: 21g; Sugar: 16g; Protein: 23g

CHEESY BROCCOLI OAT-SOTTO

SERVES 2 | **PREP TIME** 10 minutes | **COOK TIME** 40 minutes

Oatmeal leaves its comfort zone as a breakfast staple and makes its debut as a dinner entrée. This recipe will have you seriously rethinking your relationship with the humble oat. A hybrid of oatmeal and cheddar-broccoli soup that resembles risotto may not sound like an obvious go-to, but give it a try and you'll be hooked. Plus, you get the taste of risotto without the stirring and time commitment.

1 tablespoon olive oil (optional)

½ cup diced yellow or white onion

1 garlic clove, finely minced

1½ cups Cheesy Sauce (page 112)

2½ cups Quick Umami Broth (page 110), or store-bought low-sodium vegetable broth

1 cup steel-cut oats

2 cups chopped frozen broccoli

¼ cup nutritional yeast

Sea salt (optional)

Freshly ground black pepper

1. Preheat a medium nonstick saucepan over medium-low heat for 5 minutes.

2. Pour in the oil (if using) and add the onion and garlic to the pan. Cook for about 5 minutes, stirring frequently, until the onion has softened.

3. Add the cheesy sauce and broth and bring the mixture to a boil over medium-high heat.

4. Stir in the oats and cook for about 20 minutes, or until the oats are just tender.

5. Stir in the broccoli and nutritional yeast, bring to a simmer over medium-high heat, and cook for 5 minutes. Season with salt (if using) and pepper to taste and serve immediately.

SOS-FREE TIP: Sauté the aromatics with 2 tablespoons of vegetable broth rather than using olive oil. Skip the salt.

PER SERVING (3 CUPS): Calories: 550; Fat: 10g; Sodium: 384mg; Carbohydrates: 91g; Fiber: 22g; Sugar: 9g; Protein: 31g

CURRIED LENTIL AND BUTTERNUT SQUASH HARVEST BOWL

SERVES 2 | **PREP TIME** 15 minutes | **COOK TIME** 25 minutes

This dish balances the warmth of curry spices with the sweetness of butternut squash to create a hearty bowl of plant-based goodness for that chilly fall evening. Get creative and experiment with different curry blends, add more vegetables like diced zucchini or riced cauliflower, or wilt in some leafy greens in the final step before serving.

2 cups Quick Umami Broth (page 110), or store-bought low-sodium vegetable broth

½ cup quinoa, rinsed

2 tablespoons almond butter

1½ cups water

1 tablespoon olive oil

½ cup diced yellow or white onion

1 garlic clove, finely minced

1½ teaspoons curry powder

½ cup dried green, French, or black lentils, rinsed and sorted (See Mushroom, Lentil, and Spinach Stew, Cooking tip, page 51) ▸

1. In a medium nonstick saucepan, bring the broth to a boil over medium-high heat. Stir in the quinoa and simmer for 15 to 20 minutes, or until the quinoa is tender.

2. While the quinoa cooks, in a blender, combine the almond butter and water and blend until smooth.

3. Preheat a medium nonstick saucepan over medium-low heat for 5 minutes.

4. Pour in the oil and add the onion, garlic, and curry powder. Cook for 3 to 5 minutes, stirring frequently, until the onion is softened and the garlic and spices are aromatic. Add the almond butter mixture to the saucepan, bring the contents to a rolling boil, stir in the lentils and butternut squash, and simmer for 15 minutes, or until the lentils are tender.

2 cups cubed (½ inch) peeled butternut squash (from 1 small butternut squash)

½ cup chopped fresh cilantro

Sea salt

Freshly ground black pepper

5. Remove the curry mixture from the heat, gently fold in the cilantro, season with salt and pepper to taste, and serve over the quinoa.

COOKING TIP: Reduce prep time by purchasing precut butternut squash in your market's produce section, or substitute frozen butternut squash. If you can't find butternut squash, use sweet potato.

PER SERVING (2 CUPS): Calories: 628; Fat: 20g; Sodium: 190mg; Carbohydrates: 95g; Fiber: 24g; Sugar: 12g; Protein: 25g

UNWRAPPED SAMOSA BOWL

SERVES 2 | **PREP TIME** 10 minutes | **COOK TIME** 20 minutes

The triangular fried pastry practically synonymous with Indian cuisine does not have to be completely ruled out of a plant-based lifestyle. Skip the grease and get ready for a lighter, faster, and easier way to enjoy the flavors of samosas in fewer than 30 minutes.

3 cups cubed (¾ inch) Yukon Gold potatoes (from 2 or 3 potatoes)

2 tablespoons olive oil, divided

½ cup diced yellow or white onion

1 garlic clove, finely minced

¼ teaspoon sea salt

1 teaspoon garam masala or curry powder

⅛ teaspoon chili powder

1 large carrot, grated

1½ cups frozen peas, thawed

¼ cup chopped fresh cilantro

Freshly ground black pepper

1. In a medium nonstick saucepan, combine the potatoes with enough water to cover and bring to a rolling boil over high heat. Reduce the heat to medium-low and simmer for about 10 minutes, or until the potatoes are just tender when pierced with the tip of a paring knife. Drain the potatoes and toss them with 1 tablespoon of oil to coat thoroughly. Set aside.

2. While the potatoes cook, preheat a large nonstick skillet over medium-low heat for 5 minutes.

3. Pour in the remaining 1 tablespoon of oil and add the onion, garlic, salt, garam masala, chili powder, and carrot. Cook for about 3 minutes, stirring frequently, or until the onion is tender and slightly browned and the garlic and spices are fragrant.

4. Add the peas to the skillet and cook for 3 minutes.

5. Add the potatoes and gently stir to combine. Cook over medium-low heat for 3 to 4 minutes, or until the potatoes are slightly browned.

6. Remove the pot from the heat, stir in the cilantro, and season with more salt and pepper to taste.

PER SERVING (2 CUPS): Calories: 396; Fat: 14g; Sodium: 500mg; Carbohydrates: 63g; Fiber: 11g; Sugar: 11g; Protein: 10g

LEMONY PICCATA POTATO SALAD

SERVES 2 | **PREP TIME** 10 minutes | **COOK TIME** 15 minutes

This potato salad recipe would have you boasting the blue ribbon at any state-fair contest. Banish from your mind images of potatoes swamped in mayonnaise and get ready to try this hearty, bright, flavorful version.

3 cups scrubbed and cubed (¾ inch) Yukon Gold potatoes (from 2 or 3 potatoes)

1 cup Savory Nut and Seed Cream Sauce (page 117), or store-bought plant-based Alfredo sauce (like Primal Kitchen)

1 medium garlic clove, finely minced

Juice of 1 lemon

Grated zest of 1 lemon

1½ tablespoons capers, drained and chopped

⅓ cup chopped fresh parsley

2 scallions, white and green parts, finely chopped

1 (15-ounce) can no-salt-added chickpeas, drained and rinsed

1 cup finely chopped fresh baby greens, such as baby spinach or kale

Sea salt

Freshly ground black pepper

1. In a medium nonstick saucepan, combine the potatoes with enough water to cover and bring to a rolling boil over high heat. Reduce the heat to medium-low and simmer for about 10 minutes, or until the potatoes are just tender when pierced with the tip of a paring knife. Drain the potatoes and set aside.

2. In a large salad bowl, whisk the cream sauce, garlic, lemon juice, lemon zest, and capers to blend. Stir in the parsley, scallions, chickpeas, and greens.

3. Add the potatoes to the salad bowl while still warm, and gently stir to coat thoroughly. Season with salt and pepper to taste and serve warm, or refrigerate in an airtight container for up to 3 days and serve cold.

VARIATION TIP: Get adventurous and add some finely minced green or red chiles. Have some fun experimenting with different herbs, like fresh oregano or tarragon. Can't find capers? Green olives are a great substitute.

PER SERVING (2 CUPS): Calories: 555; Fat: 18g; Sodium: 326mg; Carbohydrates: 87g; Fiber: 18g; Sugar: 8g; Protein: 22g

QUICK MUSHROOM AND KALE RISOTTO

SERVES 2 | **PREP TIME** 10 minutes | **COOK TIME** 45 minutes

Traditional risotto recipes use arborio rice, a starchy processed white rice that requires almost constant stirring for what feels like AGES. This recipe uses wholesome brown rice instead and lets my Savory Nut and Seed Cream Sauce (page 117) do the heavy lifting to make the rice rich and creamy without the time investment or the saturated fat typically added by butter and heavy cream. If you like to make extra batches of brown rice, this recipe can get dinner on the table even more quickly.

2 cups water

1 cup brown rice

1 tablespoon olive oil

1 medium garlic clove, finely minced

1/2 medium white or yellow onion, diced

1/8 teaspoon red pepper flakes

Sea salt

3 cups sliced washed white or brown button mushrooms

3 cups chopped stemmed fresh kale leaves ▶

1. In a medium nonstick pan with a tight-fitting lid, bring the water to a boil. Stir in the rice and bring the water back to a boil. Cover the pan, reduce the heat to medium-low, and gently simmer for about 40 minutes, or until the rice is tender.

2. While the rice cooks, preheat a large nonstick skillet over medium heat for 5 minutes.

3. Pour in the oil and add the garlic, onion, red pepper flakes, and a pinch of salt. Cook for about 3 minutes, stirring frequently, or until the onion has softened and is translucent.

4. Add the mushrooms to the skillet, turn the heat to medium-high, and cook for about 10 minutes, or until most of the mushrooms' moisture has released into the skillet and evaporated. Add the kale and cook for about 5 minutes, stirring frequently, until tender and wilted,

1 cup Savory Nut and Seed Cream Sauce (page 117), or store-bought plant-based Alfredo sauce (like Primal Kitchen)

1 cup Quick Umami Broth (page 110), or store-bought low-sodium vegetable broth, as needed

Freshly ground black pepper

5. Stir in the cooked rice and cream sauce until combined thoroughly. A few tablespoons at a time, stir in the broth until the dish is creamy and has a porridgelike consistency. Bring the risotto to a simmer over medium-high heat and cook for 2 to 3 minutes. Season with black pepper to taste and serve immediately.

COOKING TIP: Cut your prep time in half by buying prewashed chopped kale and prewashed sliced mushrooms.

SOS-FREE TIP: Omit the oil and use 2 tablespoons of vegetable broth to prevent the garlic and onion from burning and sticking to the pan.

PER SERVING (2 CUPS): Calories: 583; Fat: 25g; Sodium: 175mg; Carbohydrates: 83g; Fiber: 10g; Sugar: 8g; Protein: 19g

LENTIL AND QUINOA PESTO POWER BOWL

SERVES 2 | **PREP TIME** 15 minutes | **COOK TIME** 40 minutes

Between the high protein and fiber in the lentils, the fiber and antioxidants in the quinoa, the vitamin wealth of the spinach, and the iron, magnesium, and vitamin K in the pine nuts, this power bowl should really earn the title of Super Power Bowl. Add to that the rich, creamy taste of the pesto and this dish will become a regular on your dinner table.

2 cups water

1½ cups Quick Umami Broth (page 110), or store-bought low-sodium vegetable broth

½ cup dried green, French, or black lentils, rinsed and sorted (See Mushroom, Lentil, and Spinach Stew, Cooking tip, page 51)

½ cup quinoa, rinsed

½ cup Herb Pesto (page 118), or store-bought plant-based pesto

¼ medium red onion, finely chopped

2 cups finely chopped fresh spinach

2 teaspoons grated lemon zest

Freshly ground black pepper

2 tablespoons pine nuts

1. In a medium nonstick saucepan, bring the water and broth to a rolling boil. Add the lentils and quinoa, reduce the heat to medium-low, and simmer for about 25 minutes, or until the lentils and quinoa are tender. Drain the lentils and quinoa and put them in a large mixing bowl.

2. Add the pesto, onion, spinach, and lemon zest and gently fold to combine everything thoroughly. Season with pepper to taste.

3. Heat a small nonstick skillet over medium heat for 5 minutes.

4. Pour in the pine nuts and cook for 5 minutes, stirring frequently to prevent burning, or until lightly browned.

5. Divide the lentil-quinoa mixture between two bowls, garnish with toasted pine nuts, and serve slightly warm or chilled.

VARIATION TIP: Don't be shy about adding fresh herbs to this recipe. A generous handful of fresh basil, oregano, or parsley with some lemon wedges for an extra sprinkling of bright citrus flavor will give this power bowl a flavorful boost.

PER SERVING (2 CUPS): Calories: 534; Fat: 19g; Sodium: 265mg; Carbohydrates: 71g; Fiber: 17g; Sugar: 7g; Protein: 24g

SPAGHETTI WITH LENTILS AND GREENS

SERVES 2 | **PREP TIME** 10 minutes | **COOK TIME** 25 minutes

We all need our homemade spaghetti and meatballs recipe, only here we ditch the meatballs for a smaller, round ball . . . the lentil! This dish has amazing flavor, especially enhanced by the fresh herbs, but minus the fat and carbon footprint. Feel free to substitute any whole-grain or gluten-free pasta you like here.

11½ cups water, divided

¾ cup dried green, French, or black lentils, rinsed and sorted (See Mushroom, Lentil, and Spinach Stew, Cooking tip, page 51)

1½ cups Easy Marinara (page 114), or store-bought low-sodium marinara sauce

3 cups chopped stemmed Swiss chard

6 ounces dried whole-wheat spaghetti

Sea salt (optional)

Freshly ground black pepper

½ cup fresh basil, oregano, or parsley leaves

1. In a large nonstick skillet, bring 1½ cups of water to a rolling boil. Add the lentils and marinara and bring the liquid back to a boil over high heat. Reduce the heat to medium-low and gently simmer for about 20 minutes, or until the lentils are just barely tender.

2. Stir in the Swiss chard and cook for 3 to 5 minutes, until the greens have wilted. Keep warm over low heat until the pasta is ready.

3. While the lentils cook, in a large saucepan, bring the remaining 10 cups of water to a boil. Add the spaghetti and gently boil until just barely tender and still al dente, according to the package instructions. Drain the spaghetti and add it to the lentil mixture. Cook for 3 to 5 minutes over medium heat to finish cooking the pasta and let it absorb the sauce. Season with salt (if using) and pepper to taste, garnish with the basil, and serve.

VARIATION TIP: If you're a garlic lover, like I am, add 1 teaspoon of garlic powder or 1 or 2 garlic cloves, finely minced, with the Swiss chard. Can't find fresh Swiss chard in the produce section? Try the freezer aisle.

PER SERVING (2 CUPS): Calories: 597; Fat: 6g; Sodium: 151mg; Carbohydrates: 114g; Fiber: 22g; Sugar: 9g; Protein: 30g

GINGER AND CHILE EDAMAME HUMMUS PASTA

SERVES 2 | **PREP TIME** 15 minutes | **COOK TIME** 25 minutes

This dish is a bold and exciting flavor bomb. Instead of a more traditional pasta sauce, I use hummus made from edamame—immature soybeans—which are high in protein, fiber, vitamins, and minerals. Turn up the heat by keeping the seeds in the chile, or lower the spiciness with a milder pepper, like Fresno or jalapeño.

4 cups water

1 (10-ounce) bag frozen shelled edamame, thawed

2 teaspoons white miso

1 medium garlic clove, minced

2 teaspoons peeled and minced fresh ginger

1 red Thai chile, seeded and finely minced

2 tablespoons sunflower seed butter

Grated zest of 1 lime

Juice of 1 lime

½ cup chopped fresh cilantro

2 scallions, white and green parts, finely diced

6 ounces dried whole-wheat penne pasta

1. In a medium saucepan, bring the water to a rolling boil. Add the edamame and cook for about 5 minutes over high heat, or until the beans are tender. Drain the beans and cool them quickly under cold running water.

2. In a large mixing bowl, stir together the miso, garlic, ginger, chile, sunflower seed butter, lime zest, and lime juice until mixed thoroughly.

3. Add the cooled edamame and, using the back of a large serving spoon or potato masher, mash the beans into the mixture to form a thick, rustic hummus texture. Stir in the cilantro and scallions.

4. In a medium saucepan, cook the pasta according to the package instructions. Drain the pasta and reserve 1 cup of pasta water.

5. In the empty warm pasta pot, combine the hummus and ½ cup of pasta water. Bring to a gentle simmer over medium-high heat. Gently fold in the pasta, stirring and adding more pasta water, a few tablespoons at a time, to achieve a creamy consistency. Serve.

PER SERVING (2 CUPS): Calories: 625; Fat: 18g; Sodium: 221mg; Carbohydrates: 90g; Fiber: 22g; Sugar: 9g; Protein: 36g

CITRUS AND HERB CAULIFLOWER AND QUINOA BOWLS

SERVES 2 | **PREP TIME** 10 minutes | **COOK TIME** 30 minutes

Cauliflower, which is actually a flower, is packed with vitamin C and comes in four colors: green, orange, purple, and white. Bright citrus and bold herbs bring a lot of flavor to this dish without adding too much salt or any refined sugar or oil.

1½ cups Quick Umami Broth (page 110), or store-bought low-sodium vegetable broth

½ cup dried quinoa, rinsed

1 garlic clove, finely minced

1 teaspoon Dijon mustard

3 tablespoons Veggie Magic Sauce (page 111; see Variation tip)

Juice of 1 lemon

Grated zest of 1 lemon

3 cups coarsely chopped cauliflower florets (from 1 medium cauliflower)

¼ cup water

½ cup chopped fresh herbs (such as basil, dill, oregano, or parsley)

1. In a medium nonstick saucepan, bring the broth to a boil. Stir in the quinoa, cover the pan, and simmer over medium-low heat for about 20 minutes, or until the quinoa is tender. Keep warm until ready to serve.

2. While the quinoa cooks, in a small mixing bowl, stir together the garlic, mustard, veggie magic sauce, lemon juice, and lemon zest. Set aside.

3. In a medium nonstick skillet with a tight-fitting lid, arrange the cauliflower in a single layer, pour in the water, and cover the skillet. Bring to a simmer over medium heat and cook for 7 to 10 minutes, or until the cauliflower is tender and easily pierced with the tip of a paring knife.

4. Add the set-aside sauce to the skillet, toss to coat the cauliflower, and heat thoroughly over medium heat for 2 minutes. Remove the skillet from the heat and stir in the fresh herbs.

5. To serve, divide the quinoa into two bowls and top with the cauliflower.

VARIATION TIP: If you're short on time, replace the Veggie Magic Sauce (page 111) with 2 tablespoons of tahini and 1 tablespoon of freshly squeezed lemon juice.

PER SERVING (2 CUPS): Calories: 321; Fat: 10g; Sodium: 331mg; Carbohydrates: 50g; Fiber: 11g; Sugar: 10g; Protein: 12g

Strawberry and Balsamic Galette 104

Chapter Seven

DESSERTS

SWEET LEMON AND THYME POLENTA WITH CITRUS-TAHINI DRIZZLE

SERVES 2 | **PREP TIME** 20 minutes, plus 15 minutes to chill | **COOK TIME** 50 minutes

Polenta is actually more dessertlike than it may seem at first glance. Think corn pudding. You'll love how quick, easy, forgiving, and versatile this dessert is. Enjoy it any time of year by topping the polenta with seasonal fruit and a dollop of plant-based yogurt.

1½ cups water, plus more as needed

5 Medjool dates, pitted and chopped, divided

1 teaspoon white miso

1 teaspoon chopped fresh thyme leaves

¾ cup medium-grind cornmeal

Grated zest of 1 lemon

Juice of 1 lemon, divided

Grated zest of 1 lime

Juice of 1 lime

1½ tablespoons tahini

1. In a blender, combine the water, 4 dates, and the miso and blend until smooth. Transfer this mixture to a medium nonstick saucepan and bring to a boil over medium-high heat.

2. Stir the thyme and cornmeal into the boiling liquid and cook for 2 to 3 minutes, stirring, or until thickened. Reduce the heat to low and let the polenta gently simmer for 40 minutes. During the cooking time, you may need to gradually add up to an additional 1 cup of water to keep the polenta easily stirrable.

3. Remove the saucepan from the heat and stir in the lemon zest and half of the lemon juice. While still warm, pour the polenta into a 2-cup bowl, or two 1-cup bowls for single-serving portions, and refrigerate for at least 15 minutes, or until solidi-fied. This polenta can be kept covered in the fridge for up to 3 days.

4. When ready to serve, in a small mixing bowl, stir together the remaining lemon juice, the lime zest, lime juice, tahini, and the remaining date. Using the back of a fork or a spoon, smash the date into a paste and combine it with the tahini and citrus. Thin to a consistency that's easily drizzled by adding up to 1 tablespoon of water.

5. To plate the polenta, run the tip of a paring knife along the inside of the bowl to loosen the polenta and invert it onto a serving plate. Drizzle with the tahini sauce and serve.

COOKING TIP: To test whether the polenta has cooked long enough, place a spoonful on a cold plate or bowl and allow it to cool and solidify. The corn should be soft, not gritty. Dramatically reduce your cooking time by choosing "instant polenta" cornmeal and follow the package instructions.

PER SERVING (1 CUP): Calories: 462; Fat: 9g; Sodium: 104mg; Carbohydrates: 98g; Fiber: 14g; Sugar: 44g; Protein: 8g

BLUEBERRY AND PEACH CHIA PARFAITS

SERVES 2 | **PREP TIME** 30 minutes, plus 2 hours to chill

What is better than a healthy dessert that doesn't taste healthy? This pudding features chia seeds, which are an amazing source of fiber, protein, and omega-3s. Add blueberries, peaches, and walnuts and you basically have a bowl of superfoods disguised as dessert. This refreshing dessert is ideal for those hot summer days when the last thing you want to do is stand over a hot stove.

1 cup soy milk

¼ cup chia seeds

2 Medjool dates, finely chopped

1 cup fresh blueberries

1 cup chopped fresh peaches

1 tablespoon chopped walnuts (optional)

1. In a 16-ounce jar, combine the milk, chia seeds, and dates and stir to mix thoroughly. Let sit for about 20 minutes to begin thickening, then stir the mixture again to break up any seed clumps. Refrigerate for at least 2 hours.

2. When ready to serve, layer the chia pudding with the blueberries and peaches and garnish with the walnuts (if using).

VARIATION TIP: This three-ingredient chia pudding base is extremely versatile. Try adding ¼ teaspoon of vanilla extract to the pudding and serve with sliced bananas, strawberries, and shaved dairy-free dark chocolate for a fun take on a banana split.

PER SERVING (1½ CUPS): Calories: 273; Fat: 8g; Sodium: 50mg; Carbohydrates: 47g; Fiber: 13g; Sugar: 30g; Protein: 9g

PUMPKIN PIE SPICED BAKED APPLES

SERVES 2 | **PREP TIME** 15 minutes | **COOK TIME** 45 minutes

Join the pumpkin spice bandwagon without the added sugar and dairy, and relish the cozy, warm fall flavors in an easy pre portioned dessert. My favorite varieties of apple to use for this are Jonagold and Honeycrisp, but use any semi-tart, crisp apple you like. If you use a tart apple, like Granny Smith, add an extra date or two to balance the apples' tartness.

2 tablespoons finely chopped walnuts

2 tablespoons old-fashioned rolled oats

1 tablespoon raisins

1 teaspoon pumpkin pie spice

2 Medjool dates, finely chopped

1 tablespoon sunflower seed butter

2 large semi-tart apples, cored

½ cup water

1. Preheat the oven to 375°F.

2. In a small mixing bowl, stir together the walnuts, oats, raisins, pumpkin pie spice, dates, and sunflower seed butter until combined thoroughly to form the apple stuffing.

3. Place the apples in a 4-cup oven-safe baking dish and fill their hollow centers with the spiced oat mixture. Pour the water into the baking dish.

4. Bake for about 45 minutes, or until the apples are tender. Let the apples cool for at least 10 minutes before serving.

COOKING TIP: Don't have time to bake these in the oven? Cook them in a microwave-safe bowl, uncovered, on high power for 6 to 9 minutes in the microwave. Let cool for at least 5 minutes before serving.

PER SERVING (1 APPLE): Calories: 315; Fat: 10g; Sodium: 5mg; Carbohydrates: 59g; Fiber: 9g; Sugar: 43g; Protein: 4g

BANANA AND PEANUT BUTTER CHIA PUDDING

SERVES 2 | **PREP TIME** 25 minutes, plus 2 hours to chill

Take your peanut butter and banana sandwich to the next level with this make-ahead dessert even Elvis would appreciate. And what a great way to use overripe bananas. When your bananas look spotty and brown, peel them and freeze them in an airtight container for up to 1 month to use for this pudding recipe.

1 cup soy milk

2 ripe bananas, mashed

¼ cup chia seeds

2 tablespoons natural chunky peanut butter

2 tablespoons chopped dry-roasted peanuts

1. In a medium mixing bowl, whisk the milk, bananas, chia seeds, and peanut butter to combine thoroughly. Let the pudding rest and thicken for 20 minutes, then whisk it again to break up any seed clumps.

2. Divide the mixture between two Mason jars or bowls, garnish with the chopped peanuts, and refrigerate for at least 2 hours, or overnight, before serving.

VARIATION TIP: A small handful of dairy-free chocolate chips, chopped walnuts, shredded coconut, or some fresh or frozen strawberries can enhance this pudding. Swap the peanut butter for sunflower seed butter and omit the peanut garnish if you want it to be nut-free.

PER SERVING (¾ CUP): Calories: 383; Fat: 21g; Sodium: 97mg; Carbohydrates: 42g; Fiber: 14g; Sugar: 16g; Protein: 15g

BROILED STONE FRUIT WITH LEMON-PECAN DRIZZLE

SERVES 2 | **PREP TIME** 15 minutes | **COOK TIME** 5 minutes

Summer is famous for its juicy, flavorful stone fruits: Apricots, apriums, nectarines, peaches, plumcots, plums, and pluots are just some of the options to choose from. This dish works best when the fruit is ripe but not mushy, and it is next-level amazing served with a dollop of your favorite nondairy yogurt.

4 tablespoons Fruit Magic Dressing (page 113), divided

2 tablespoons freshly squeezed lemon juice

1 tablespoon pecan butter

2 stone fruits, halved and pitted

2 teaspoons finely chopped fresh basil leaves

1. Preheat the broiler for 10 minutes.

2. In a small bowl, stir together 2 tablespoons of fruit magic dressing, the lemon juice, and pecan butter and set aside.

3. Brush the stone fruit halves with 1 tablespoon of fruit magic dressing and place them, cut-side up, in a small oven-safe baking dish, evenly spaced.

4. Broil for 3 to 5 minutes, checking frequently to prevent burning.

5. Brush the broiled fruit with the remaining 1 tablespoon of dressing and let cool for 3 minutes. Garnish the fruit with the basil and serve with the lemon-pecan drizzle on the side.

COOKING TIP: No need to come inside to make dessert. Why not grill it? Clean and season your grill grates well with oil. Cook the fruit over low heat for 5 minutes per side until soft with blackened grill marks.

PER SERVING (2 HALVES AND 2 TABLESPOONS SAUCE): Calories: 160; Fat: 6g; Sodium: 31mg; Carbohydrates: 29g; Fiber: 4g; Sugar: 24g; Protein: 3g

SPICED BROWN RICE PUDDING WITH RAISINS

SERVES 2 | **PREP TIME** 5 minutes | **COOK TIME** 1 hour

You don't have to wait until National Rice Pudding Day, August 9, to enjoy this UK tradition. Create a rich, creamy dessert in a matter of minutes any time of year. Served warm or chilled, this dish is satisfying and hearty enough for breakfast or an energy-boosting snack in the afternoon. And best of all, this version features a fiber-rich, hearty, and heart-healthy whole grain.

1 cup water

½ cup brown rice

¾ cup soy milk

3 tablespoons maple syrup, or 3 Medjool dates, finely minced

½ cup raisins

1 tablespoon almond butter

½ teaspoon ground cinnamon

1. In a small nonstick saucepan, bring the water to a boil. Stir in the rice and lower the heat to medium. Simmer for 40 minutes, or until tender.

2. In a medium nonstick saucepan, combine the cooked rice, milk, maple syrup, raisins, almond butter, and cinnamon and bring to a boil over medium-high heat. Reduce the heat to medium-low and simmer for 15 to 20 minutes, stirring frequently, until thickened. Serve the pudding warm or cold.

3. Refrigerate leftovers in an airtight container for up to 5 days.

VARIATION TIP: Get creative with textures and add some shredded coconut, chopped nuts and seeds, or even diced apple.

PER SERVING (1 CUP): Calories: 413; Fat: 7g; Sodium: 45mg; Carbohydrates: 85g; Fiber: 6g; Sugar: 43g; Protein: 10g

NO-BAKE 4-INGREDIENT PECAN PIE COOKIES

SERVES 2 | **PREP TIME** 10 minutes

I daydream about pecan pie, but alas, it is a rare treat. I made this recipe to satisfy that craving, so if you're short on time and love pecan pie as much as I do, these cookies are for you. This recipe needs only a handful of ingredients and comes together in less time than it takes to preheat the oven.

¼ cup finely chopped raw pecans

2 Medjool dates, pitted and finely chopped

¼ teaspoon white miso

¼ teaspoon vanilla extract or vanilla bean powder

Raw pecan halves, for garnish (optional)

1. In a sealed plastic bag, crush the chopped pecans into a coarse powder with the bottom of a skillet or a rolling pin. Transfer the crushed nuts to a small mixing bowl and add the dates, miso, and vanilla. Using the back of a fork or spoon, mash the ingredients into a thick paste.

2. Divide the dough into two equal portions, roll each into a ball, and slightly flatten them to form two cookies. Press a raw pecan half into the top of each cookie (if using) before serving.

COOKING TIP: Double this recipe and refrigerate leftovers in an airtight container for up to 1 week.

PER SERVING (1 COOKIE): Calories: 163; Fat: 10g; Sodium: 23mg; Carbohydrates: 20g; Fiber: 3g; Sugar: 17g; Protein: 2g

STRAWBERRY AND BALSAMIC GALETTE

SERVES 2 | **PREP TIME** 15 minutes | **COOK TIME** 30 minutes

This galette (basically a free-form pie) calls for black pepper, which may seem strange to add to a dessert. But trust me on this one—the heat from the pepper actually accentuates the strawberries' natural sweetness and flavor.

½ cup canned pumpkin or sweet potato

½ cup whole-wheat flour, plus more for dusting

½ cup almond meal

3 Medjool dates, finely minced

1 teaspoon white miso

2 cups hulled and halved fresh strawberries

½ cup balsamic vinegar

⅛ teaspoon freshly ground black pepper

1. Position an oven rack in the lowest position and preheat the oven to 400°F. Line a baking sheet with parchment paper or a silicone baking mat.

2. In a large mixing bowl, thoroughly mix the pumpkin, flour, almond meal, dates, and miso until the mixture comes together into a cohesive ball.

3. Lightly dust a work surface with flour and, using a rolling pin, roll the dough on it into a 10-inch circle. Transfer the crust to the prepared baking sheet.

4. Arrange the strawberries on the crust, leaving a 1½-inch border around the edge. Fold the crust's edges over the strawberries, pleating and pinching the dough.

5. Bake on the lowest rack for 25 to 30 minutes, or until the crust is golden brown.

6. While the galette bakes, in a small nonstick saucepan, combine the balsamic vinegar and pepper and bring to a boil over medium-high heat. Reduce the heat to medium-low and simmer for about 5 minutes, until the vinegar has reduced in volume by half.

7. Using a pastry brush, apply the balsamic glaze to the strawberries. Serve warm or chilled.

PER SERVING (½ GALETTE): Calories: 492; Fat: 15g; Sodium: 120mg; Carbohydrates: 83g; Fiber: 14g; Sugar: 45g; Protein: 13g

CHERRY, WALNUT, AND DARK CHOCOLATE OATMEAL BOWL

SERVES 2 | **PREP TIME** 5 minutes | **COOK TIME** 20 minutes

The taste of this dish is reminiscent of chocolate-covered cherries, also known as cherry cordials, a candy originating in 18th-century France (called *griottes*). Although this version is alcohol-free, you'll find it just as (well, almost as) fun for a quick weeknight dessert or even a brunch treat.

1 cup soy milk

½ cup chopped walnuts, divided

1 cup water

2 tablespoons unsweetened cocoa powder

3 Medjool dates, pitted and chopped

½ teaspoon vanilla extract or vanilla bean powder

½ teaspoon white miso

1¼ cups pitted and halved fresh or frozen cherries

1 cup old-fashioned rolled oats

1. In a blender, combine the milk, 1/4 cup of walnuts, water, cocoa powder, dates, vanilla, and miso and blend until smooth. Transfer the blended mixture to a medium nonstick saucepan and bring to a boil over medium-high heat.

2. Stir in the cherries and oats, bring back to a boil, then reduce the heat to medium-low and simmer for 7 to 9 minutes, or until the oatmeal is thick and the oats are tender.

3. Garnish with the remaining ¼ cup of walnuts and serve warm or chilled.

COOKING TIP: If you have a little more time and want a more wholesome oatmeal, steel-cut oats or whole oat groats is another great choice. Use 3 cups of water to 1 cup of steel-cut oats and simmer for about 30 minutes, or use equal amounts of whole oat groats and water and simmer for 1 hour.

PER SERVING (1 CUP): Calories: 555; Fat: 25g; Sodium: 92mg; Carbohydrates: 78g; Fiber: 14g; Sugar: 37g; Protein: 17g

PEANUT BUTTER AND WINTER SQUASH MOUSSE

SERVES 2 | **PREP TIME** 5 minutes | **COOK TIME** 30 minutes, plus 1 hour to chill

This recipe was an accidental creation I made years ago, and it was so surprisingly delicious, I've never looked back. Although ideally made with kabocha squash, which has a dry, crumbly texture when roasted, butternut squash or even canned pumpkin will work in a pinch. But be forewarned: The texture will be softer and more puddinglike with these other ingredients.

1 kabocha squash

2 tablespoons natural crunchy peanut butter

¼ teaspoon vanilla extract or vanilla bean powder

Sea salt (optional)

2 tablespoons chopped dry-roasted peanuts, for garnish

1. Preheat the oven to 425°F. Line a baking sheet with parchment paper or a silicone baking mat.

2. Carefully halve the squash and scoop out the seeds. Arrange the squash halves, cut-side down, on a cutting board and cut them into 1-inch slices. Place the slices on the prepared baking sheet, evenly spaced.

3. Roast for 15 minutes. Flip each piece and roast for 15 minute more, or until the squash is easily pierced with the tip of a paring knife. Let the roasted squash cool, then scoop the flesh out of the skins with a spoon and measure out 2 cups of roasted squash.

4. In a medium mixing bowl, using an electric hand mixer or wire whisk, combine thoroughly the roasted kabocha, peanut butter, vanilla, and salt (if using) to taste. It's best (but not mandatory) if you refrigerate the mousse for 1 hour before serving, garnished with the chopped peanuts. This mousse can also be made up to 2 days in advance and refrigerated in an airtight container until ready to serve.

COOKING TIP: The squash is roasted with the skin on. Let the roasted squash cool, then scoop the flesh out of the skin with a spoon and measure out the amount you need.

VARIATION TIP: This recipe also makes deliciously unusual popsicles, especially if you use canned pumpkin, which will create a softer-textured dessert. Add the mixture to ice-pop molds and freeze overnight for a sweet, creamy treat.

PER SERVING (1 CUP): Calories: 201; Fat: 13g; Sodium: 1mg; Carbohydrates: 15g; Fiber: 3g; Sugar: 5g; Protein: 8g

Left to right: Easy Marinara, page 114; Herb Pesto, page 118; and Cheesy Sauce, page 112

Chapter Eight

STAPLES

QUICK UMAMI BROTH

MAKES about 4 cups | **PREP TIME** 10 minutes | **COOK TIME** 20 minutes

Most store-bought vegetable broths are loaded with added sodium and don't compare favorably to the flavor of homemade broths. This delicious broth uses only a handful of healthy ingredients and doesn't require hours of simmering on the stovetop. I always keep a batch of this broth in the fridge to whip up a quick and easy soup, like my Ginger, Peanut, and Carrot Bisque (page 47), or to boost flavor when used instead of water in recipes like my Versatile Vegetable Rice Pilaf (page 37).

4½ cups water

1 carrot, washed and grated

1 small onion, finely chopped

1 celery stalk, finely chopped

½ ounce dried shiitake mushrooms, or 5 or 6 fresh shiitake mushroom caps

1 teaspoon tomato paste

1 tablespoon red miso

1. In a medium nonstick saucepan, thoroughly mix the water, carrot, onion, celery, mushrooms, tomato paste, and miso and bring to a boil over medium-high heat. Reduce the heat to medium-low and simmer for 15 minutes.

2. Set a fine-mesh sieve over a heatproof bowl and strain the solids from the broth. Discard the solids. Refrigerate the broth in an airtight container for up to 2 weeks.

COOKING TIP: As you prep vegetables throughout the week, refrigerate your vegetable trimmings, like basil, cilantro, or parsley stems or carrot, onion, or sweet potato peels, and add a handful to the saucepan here to add more complexity and flavor to your broth. Avoid adding sulfur-rich vegetables, such as broccoli, cauliflower, and kale, because they can add a bitter flavor.

PER SERVING (1 CUP): Calories: 22; Fat: <1g; Sodium: 171mg; Carbohydrates: 4g; Fiber: 1g; Sugar: 1g; Protein: 1g

VEGGIE MAGIC SAUCE

MAKES about ⅓ cup | **PREP TIME** 20 minutes

Don't let your plain veggies get you down. A little magic and—whether raw, steamed, or roasted—they can be transformed into a flavorful dish you'll actually crave. Make it once and you will quickly discover why this sauce makes the veggies disappear from the plate quickly. I always add a batch (or two) of this sauce to my weekly prep list, so I always have it on hand.

2 tablespoons tahini

Juice of 1 lemon

Grated zest of 1 lemon

1 small garlic clove, minced

1 teaspoon white miso

Freshly ground black pepper

In a small bowl, whisk the tahini, lemon juice, lemon zest, garlic, miso, and pepper to taste until blended. Set aside for 10 to 15 minutes. The sauce will thicken as the tahini absorbs the lemon juice. Adjust the sauce to your desired consistency with a little water, adding 1 tablespoon at a time. The ideal consistency is that of a creamy salad dressing. Refrigerate in an airtight container for up to 2 weeks.

USE IT AGAIN: This sauce is the key to many dishes throughout this book, such as Lemony Spring Vegetable and Farro Bowl (page 78), Citrus and Herb Cauliflower and Quinoa Bowls (page 93), and the Quick Chickpea Falafel Burgers (page 68).

VARIATION TIP: Stir in some chopped fresh herbs to brighten up steamed veggies, add a generous pinch of red pepper flakes for a spicy kick, or add a dollop of plant-based yogurt to turn this sauce into a versatile veggie dip.

PER SERVING (2 TABLESPOONS): Calories: 103; Fat: 8g; Sodium: 108mg; Carbohydrates: 7g; Fiber: 2g; Sugar: 2g; Protein: 3g

CHEESY SAUCE

MAKES about 4 cups | **PREP TIME** 10 minutes | **COOK TIME** 20 minutes

A plant-based diet does not mean the loss of that delicious cheesy taste and texture so many of us crave. In fact, I deliberately doubled this recipe to make four servings because it is so good on so many things. Try it as a sauce drizzled over steamed vegetables, and use it as the base for my Mac and Cheese with Wilted Greens (page 79) or Cheesy Broccoli Oat-sotto (page 83).

1 Yukon Gold potato, cut into ½-inch cubes

2 medium garlic cloves, chopped

1 carrot, peeled and cut into ⅛-inch-thick slices

1 small white or yellow onion, chopped

1 celery stalk, finely diced

¼ cup raw cashews

¼ cup nutritional yeast

1 tablespoon white miso

Sea salt (optional)

Freshly ground black pepper

1. In a medium nonstick saucepan, combine the potato, garlic, carrot, onion, celery, and cashews. Add just enough water to cover the vegetables. Place the saucepan over medium-high heat and bring to a boil. Reduce the heat to medium-low and simmer for about 15 minutes, or until the vegetables are tender.

2. Carefully transfer the cooked vegetables and about 1½ cups of the cooking liquid to a blender. Add the nutritional yeast and miso and blend until smooth. Season with salt (if using) and pepper to taste.

3. Refrigerate in an airtight container for up to 1 week.

USE IT AGAIN: Add the juice and grated zest of 1 lemon and 1 tablespoon of fresh dill for a surprisingly light alternative to hollandaise sauce, as I do in my Lemon and Dill Broiled Tofu (page 24), or add some salsa, diced jalapeños, and fresh cilantro to turn this sauce into a zesty queso sauce for my Veggie Nacho Platter for Two (page 34).

PER SERVING (1 CUP): Calories: 259; Fat: 8g; Sodium: 321mg; Carbohydrates: 35g; Fiber: 9g; Sugar: 7g; Protein: 16g

FRUIT MAGIC DRESSING

MAKES about ¾ cup | **PREP TIME** 10 minutes

If you're a fan of my Veggie Magic Sauce (page 111), just you wait. More magic is coming your way with this easy, healthy, delicious sauce that makes any fruit shine. It's an amazing topping for apples, berries, citrus, melons, and pears and is a fun way to season a fruit salad or add a punch of flavor to plain plant-based yogurt.

4 Medjool dates, pitted and chopped

1 teaspoon white miso

1 tablespoon chopped fresh mint leaves

½ cup water

3 tablespoons freshly squeezed lemon juice

1 teaspoon grated lemon zest

Freshly ground black pepper (optional)

In a blender, combine the dates, miso, mint, water, lemon juice, lemon zest, and pepper (if using) to taste and blend until smooth. Refrigerate in an airtight container for up to 1 week.

COOKING TIP: This recipe makes four servings, so pour any leftovers into an ice-cube tray and freeze this sauce for up to 1 month.

PER SERVING (3 TABLESPOONS): Calories: 72; Fat: <1g; Sodium: 46mg; Carbohydrates: 19g; Fiber: 2g; Sugar: 17g; Protein: 1g

EASY MARINARA

MAKES about 2 cups | **PREP TIME** 5 minutes | **COOK TIME** 20 minutes

It is said that marinara sauce, named after Italian soldiers, got its name because the ingredients—tomato, oil, garlic, dried herbs—traveled well, didn't spoil on long trips, and could be made easily in about the same amount of time that the pasta cooked. Whatever its origins, this delectable sauce has quite the following around the world. And it's versatile—whether in a simple pasta dish or served over my Sun-Dried Tomato and Herb Polenta Cakes (page 26). This version brings big tomato flavor without the added sodium and processed ingredients often found in jarred sauces.

1 (15-ounce) can no-salt-added diced tomatoes

2 teaspoons tomato paste

1 garlic clove, finely minced

1 teaspoon dried Italian seasoning

1 teaspoon extra-virgin olive oil

Sea salt (optional)

Freshly ground black pepper

In a small nonstick saucepan, combine the tomatoes and their juices, tomato paste, garlic, Italian seasoning, and oil. Place the pan over medium heat and bring to a simmer. Cook for 15 minutes to allow the herbs and garlic to infuse the sauce with their flavors. Season with salt (if using) and pepper to taste. Refrigerate in an airtight container for up to 1 week.

VARIATION TIP: If you love garlic as much as I do, add another clove or two, minced, to this recipe. Prefer a spicier sauce? Add a pinch of red pepper flakes for some extra heat. Use an immersion blender right in the pan if you like a smoother texture.

PER SERVING (1 CUP): Calories: 81; Fat: 2g; Sodium: 30mg; Carbohydrates: 12g; Fiber: 4g; Sugar: 6g; Protein: 2g

5-MINUTE TOMATO SALSA

MAKES about 2 cups | **PREP TIME** 5 minutes

Although my Summer Blueberry and Tomato Salsa (page 36) is perfect for summertime, this pantry-friendly salsa recipe is fast and easy to make year-round. Get your hands in the bowl and really mix up the ingredients to create a wonderfully rustic texture. If you prefer a smoother salsa—and cleaner hands—use a food processor or blender.

1 (15-ounce) can no-salt-added crushed tomatoes, drained

¼ cup finely chopped fresh cilantro leaves and stems

2 tablespoons finely minced jalapeño pepper

2 tablespoons freshly squeezed lime juice

1 garlic clove, minced

Sea salt (optional)

Freshly ground black pepper

In a medium mixing bowl, combine the tomatoes, cilantro, jalapeño, lime juice, and garlic and season with salt (if using) and pepper to taste. Using your hands (wear gloves if you are sensitive to chile peppers), squeeze together and massage the ingredients for 2 minutes. Pour the salsa into a fine-mesh sieve and let the excess liquid drain for about 2 minutes. Refrigerate the salsa in an airtight container for up to 1 week.

USE IT AGAIN: You'll see this fast and easy salsa recipe used in my Veggie Nacho Platter for Two (page 34) and it is a delicious addition to my Tofu Scramble with Wilted Greens (page 18).

PER SERVING (1 CUP): Calories: 62; Fat: <1g; Sodium: 28mg; Carbohydrates: 13g; Fiber: 4g; Sugar: 6g; Protein: 2g

TOMATO AND HERB DRESSING

MAKES about 1½ cups | **PREP TIME** 10 minutes

You'll ditch supermarket dressings and abandon that old boring oil and vinegar for this lovely, light dressing. It packs a flavorful punch and is even better when it's had a chance to sit overnight in the fridge. Once you try it on my Roasted Summer Vegetable Sandwiches (page 65), you'll want to keep a jar of this dressing in the fridge and at the ready for any impromptu salad.

2 Roma tomatoes, cored and coarsely chopped

1 teaspoon Dijon mustard

1 medium garlic clove, minced

1 teaspoon white miso

½ teaspoon dried Italian seasoning

¼ cup red wine vinegar

2 tablespoons balsamic vinegar

¼ cup raw sunflower seeds

Freshly ground black pepper

In a blender, combine the tomatoes, mustard, garlic, miso, Italian seasoning, red wine and balsamic vinegars, sunflower seeds, and pepper to taste. Blend until smooth. Refrigerate in an airtight container for up to 10 days.

VARIATION TIP: Swap the tomato for red bell pepper, and add a spicy kick with a pinch of red pepper flakes.

PER SERVING (6 TABLESPOONS): Calories: 71; Fat: 5g; Sodium: 80mg; Carbohydrates: 5g; Fiber: 1g; Sugar: 2g; Protein: 3g

SAVORY NUT AND SEED CREAM SAUCE

MAKES 2 cups | **PREP TIME** 10 minutes

When I kicked dairy to the curb more than a decade ago, I really wanted to create a dish that felt and tasted rich and creamy but that didn't rely on all that butter and heavy cream. Here it is. This deceptively creamy sauce uses heart-healthy seeds and nuts to bring the richness. I recommend making this in a double batch (this recipe serves four), so you can enjoy it throughout the week as a quick pasta sauce or dip, or in my Garlic Mashed Root Vegetables (page 38) or my Creamy Garlic Sautéed Greens (page 41).

1½ cups Quick Umami Broth (page 110), or store-bought low-sodium vegetable broth

½ teaspoon dried Italian seasoning

¼ cup raw sunflower seeds

2 tablespoons chopped almonds

2 tablespoons chopped raw cashews

2 tablespoons chopped walnuts

2 tablespoons raw pumpkin seeds

1 tablespoon chopped Brazil nuts

Freshly ground black pepper

In a high-speed blender (see tip), combine the broth, Italian seasoning, sunflower seeds, almonds, cashews, walnuts, pumpkin seeds, and Brazil nuts. Season with pepper to taste and blend until velvety smooth. Refrigerate in an airtight container for up to 5 days.

COOKING TIP: This recipe is designed for high-speed blenders. If you don't have a high-speed blender, place the nuts and seeds in a heatproof bowl, cover with boiling water, and let soak to soften for about 1 hour. Drain the water from the nuts and seeds before adding them to the blender with the other ingredients.

PER SERVING (½ CUP): Calories: 165; Fat: 14g; Sodium: 66mg; Carbohydrates: 7g; Fiber: 2g; Sugar: 1g; Protein: 6g

HERB PESTO

MAKES 1½ cups | **PREP TIME** 25 minutes | **COOK TIME** 5 minutes

Make your pesto completely authentic using a mortar and pestle like they did in ancient Rome. It's a little more labor intensive, but the flavor from the pulverized herbs and greens is far superior and worth the elbow grease. This pesto is clean, full of heart-healthy nuts, and not loaded with oil and salt like many supermarket counterparts. Plus, this pesto recipe blanches the herbs and greens before blending to ensure their color stays bright and vibrant.

2 cups lightly packed fresh basil leaves

2 cups lightly packed fresh baby spinach leaves

½ cup whole parsley leaves

¼ cup raw pumpkin seeds

¼ cup roughly chopped walnuts

2 tablespoons extra-virgin olive oil, plus more for storing

1 tablespoon white miso

Freshly ground black pepper

1. Fill a large bowl with ice and cold water and set aside.

2. Bring a large pot of water to a rolling boil. Drop in the basil, spinach, and parsley and submerge for 10 to 15 seconds until the leaves wilt. Using tongs or a large, slotted spoon, immediately remove the herbs and greens from the boiling water and plunge them into the ice bath to stop the cooking and preserve their bright-green color. Once cooled, remove the greens from the ice bath and pat them dry on a clean kitchen towel or with paper towels.

3. Roughly chop the blanched greens and place them in a large mortar. Add the pumpkin seeds, walnuts, oil, miso, and pepper to taste. Grind the ingredients into a smooth paste with the pestle.

4. To store this pesto and ensure it stays green, place it in an airtight container and cover the pesto with a thin layer of oil to slow the oxidation and browning process. Refrigerate for up to 1 week, or freeze for up to 1 month.

PER SERVING (6 TABLESPOONS): Calories: 166; Fat: 15g; Sodium: 153mg; Carbohydrates: 5g; Fiber: 3g; Sugar: 1g; Protein: 5g

TOFU SOUR CREAM

MAKES about 1 cup | **PREP TIME** 10 minutes

When you find yourself needing just that little dollop of sour cream for baked potatoes, burritos, or my Veggie Nacho Platter for Two (page 34), don't reach for the saturated fat–filled dairy version. This dairy-free recipe comes together in just a few minutes and tastes just as good.

1 (12-ounce) package lite firm silken tofu

2 tablespoons freshly squeezed lemon juice

1 tablespoon apple cider vinegar

1 garlic clove, minced

1 teaspoon white miso

In a blender, combine the tofu, lemon juice, vinegar, garlic, and miso and blend until velvety smooth, 1 to 2 minutes. Refrigerate in an airtight container for up to 10 days.

COOKING TIP: You can typically find silken tofu on the shelf in the international section of most supermarkets. Keep a box or two on hand to blend into creamy sauces or even desserts and smoothies for extra protein.

USE IT AGAIN: Stir in some nutritional yeast, chopped fresh chives, and a pinch each of cayenne pepper, garlic powder, and onion powder for a quick onion dip for chips and raw veggie platters.

PER SERVING (¼ CUP): Calories: 38; Fat: 1g; Sodium: 118mg; Carbohydrates: 2g; Fiber: <1g; Sugar: 1g; Protein: 6g

MEASUREMENT CONVERSIONS

VOLUME EQUIVALENTS	US STANDARD	US STANDARD (ounces)	METRIC (approximate)
LIQUID	2 tablespoons	1 fl. oz.	30 mL
	¼ cup	2 fl. oz.	60 mL
	½ cup	4 fl. oz.	120 mL
	1 cup	8 fl. oz.	240 mL
	1½ cups	12 fl. oz.	355 mL
	2 cups or 1 pint	16 fl. oz.	475 mL
	4 cups or 1 quart	32 fl. oz.	1 L
	1 gallon	128 fl. oz.	4 L
DRY	⅛ teaspoon	——————	0.5 mL
	¼ teaspoon	——————	1 mL
	½ teaspoon	——————	2 mL
	¾ teaspoon	——————	4 mL
	1 teaspoon	——————	5 mL
	1 tablespoon	——————	15 mL
	¼ cup	——————	59 mL
	⅓ cup	——————	79 mL
	½ cup	——————	118 mL
	⅔ cup	——————	156 mL
	¾ cup	——————	177 mL
	1 cup	——————	235 mL
	2 cups or 1 pint	——————	475 mL
	3 cups	——————	700 mL
	4 cups or 1 quart	——————	1 L
	½ gallon	——————	2 L
	1 gallon	——————	4 L
WEIGHT EQUIVALENTS	½ ounce	——————	15 g
	1 ounce	——————	30 g
	2 ounces	——————	60 g
	4 ounces	——————	115 g
	8 ounces	——————	225 g
	12 ounces	——————	340 g
	16 ounces or 1 pound	——————	455 g

OVEN TEMPERATURES	FAHRENHEIT (F)	CELSIUS (C) (approximate)
	250°F	120°C
	300°F	150°C
	325°F	180°C
	375°F	190°C
	400°F	200°C
	425°F	220°C
	450°F	230°C

RESOURCES

Online

NutritionFacts.org: A science-based free public online service featuring the latest in plant-based nutrition research

NutritionStudies.org: Offering plant-based eating guides and nutrition research

Physicians Committee for Responsible Medicine: Nonprofit research and advocacy organization that promotes a plant-based diet, preventive medicine, and alternatives to animal research and encourages what it describes as "higher standards of ethics and effectiveness in research"; PCRM.org

Magazines

Forks Over Knives: ForksOverKnives.com

Thrive: ThriveMagazine.com

Vegan Food and Living: VeganFoodandLiving.com

VegNews: VegNews.com

Movies

Fat, Sick, and Nearly Dead (2011)

Forks Over Knives (2011)

Hungry For Change (2012)

PlantPure Nation (2015)

The Game Changers (2018)

What the Health (2017)

Shopping

Find a **community supported agriculture** (CSA) farm program near you: LocalHarvest.org/csa/

HappyCow.net: Online plant-based local restaurant finder (think: Yelp for veggie lovers!)

National Farmers Market Directory: www.AMS.USDA.gov/local-food-directories /farmersmarkets

REFERENCES

Wansink, Brian, and Sobal, Jeffery. "Mindless Eating: The 200 Daily Food Decisions We Overlook." *Environment and Behavior* 39 (January 2007): 106–123. DOI:10.1177 /0013916506295573.

INDEX

Acknowledgments

I would like to thank:

My best friend, confidant, partner, and recipe tester/taster extraordinaire, L.L. Eveland. I wouldn't be where I am today without your unconditional love and support. My coaching clients, who continually inspire me to live by example with self-compassion, empathy, equanimity, and a sense of humor. The amazing team of health coaches I have had the honor to work with, learn from, and wholeheartedly adore: Abby Cooper, Brittany J. Stroup, Min Morris, Kimberly Whitner, Katie Sims, Katie Schultz, Anne Knott, Rachel R. White, Darielle Pickett, Hayley Whear, Jaclyn Tain, Julie Patel, and Patti Watson. Your advice, friendship, support, and understanding mean the world to me. My mother, who toiled tirelessly to find new ways to get me to eat my vegetables as a child. Your patience and perseverance paid off, and I'm infinitely grateful for the opportunity to pay it forward with this book.

About the Author

 **Sara Speckels, NBC-HWC,** is a former cell biologist turned National Board Certified Health and Wellness Coach and the creative mind behind *Farmacy Revolution*, an online resource for those looking to take their cooking, habits, and lifestyle to the next level while living a limitless and vibrant life. From growing up a confessed vegetable hater to becoming vegetables' number-one fan, it's Sara's mission to make people fall in love with the delicious and exciting world of eating more plants. When she's not cooking up a storm in the kitchen, catering whole-food, plant-based pop-up dinner parties, browsing the local farmers' markets, or coaching a client on the path to a healthier way of life, you'll likely find her paddle boarding, growing vegetables in her garden, playing with her chihuahua, Baba, hiking and foraging for wild edible plants in the woods, or training for her next half marathon.

CPSIA information can be obtained
at www.ICGtesting.com
Printed in the USA
JSHW011927051021
19327JS00001B/4